Sachiyo Ishii

Mini Knitted Woodland

Cute & easy knitting patterns for animals, birds & other forest life

Search Press

First published in 2015

Search Press Limited
Wellwood, North Farm Road,
Tunbridge Wells, Kent TN2 3DR

Reprinted 2015, 2017

Text copyright © Sachiyo Ishii, 2015

Photographs by Paul Bricknell at Search Press Studios

Photographs and design copyright © Search Press Ltd
2015

Print ISBN: 978 1 78221 068 9

Acknowledgements

I would like to thank everyone in the
Search Press team, especially Katie French and
Becky Shackleton for helping me to create such
a fantastic book. I would also like to thank the
designer, Juan Hayward, and the photographer,
Paul Bricknell, for the beautiful layout and
photography, and last but not least the pattern
checker, Jacky Edwards, for all her work.

Suppliers
If you have difficulty in obtaining any of the materials
and equipment mentioned in this book, then please
visit the Search Press website for details of suppliers:
www.searchpress.com

You are invited to view the author's work at:
etsy.com/shop/sachiyoishii
visit her website at: knitsbysachi.com
visit her blog at: knitsbysachi.wordpress.com
search for KnitsbySachi on www.ravelry.com
or search for Knits by Sachi on Facebook

Printed in China through Asia Pacific Offset

Contents

Brown bear and cubs

Racoon

Boar and piglets

Badger

Moose

Stag and doe

Fawn

Duck

Blue tit

Robin and chicks

Woodpecker

Hare

Beaver

Skunk

Fox

Otter

Wolf

Swan and cygnets

Peacock

Eagle

Stork

Owl

Hedgehog

Mouse

Squirrel

Mole

Turtle

Introduction

After creating all the animals for my first book, *Mini Knitted Safari*, it felt very natural for me to move on to woodland creatures. Many of us are familiar with a lot of woodland animals, as we grow up reading about them in stories. We sense their presence fairly often, even if we live in towns or cities, with a glimpse of a fox here and a hedgehog there, but many of these creatures are shy; I wanted to bring even the most elusive of them to life. I grew up in the countryside in Japan and, even though I had heard many tales of racoons as a child, I believed for many years that they were fictitious animals as I had never seen one!

When I started this book I knitted randomly at first, following my instincts, and soon my work table was full of little creatures. These animals seem to converse with each other, as if they lived in their own little fairy tale world, and they made me smile. So, I added a tree, a tree stump and a gnome. I soon became more and more absorbed in this project and found myself making the elements for a whole woodland scene. Along with the gnome, tree and tree stump, this book contains the designs for over twenty-seven small and medium-sized animals, which are all knitted flat and sewn together at the end. You don't need a lot of yarn at all – even an amount as small as 5g (¹/₆oz) can be transformed into a cute little creature.

You could make these animals to accompany bedtime stories for children or they could be made for charities and fundraising. There is no need to make the entire set. One or two animals can sit on your desk or perch by the window, or you could use one of them to create a little dangling charm to hang on your bag. There are many ways to enjoy them. It was such a pleasure to create this book and I hope you enjoy it as much as I did. Happy knitting!

Materials and tools

Yarn

All the animals in this book are knitted with DK (8-ply) yarn. You don't need a lot of yarn to create each animal; the average is about 5g (¹⁄₆oz), which is equivalent to a skein of tapestry wool. Even the largest, the adult bear (see pages 28–29), requires less than 10g (¹⁄₃oz). You may already have oddments of yarn left over from previous projects, so make good use of your stash if you can. When you require more than 4g (¹⁄₈oz) for a project the measurement is given in the materials list; less than 4g (¹⁄₈oz) and it is simply referred to as 'a small amount'.

I have mainly used 100 per cent wool yarns in the projects, as I love the feel of wool and the colour tones it can create. If you are making animals as children's toys, you might wish to choose natural materials. However, if you are allergic to sheep's wool, choose cotton or synthetic yarns. Tapestry yarn is fairly tightly plied and it gives a clean, finished look. Embroidery or tapestry yarns are an economical choice if you want small quantities of many different colours. Use 4-ply (fingering) yarn for embroidering faces and body markings. If you do not have any of this, simply separate out a few strands from a length of DK (8-ply) yarn. You will also need some strong cotton sewing thread, for tying up pompoms.

Stuffing

To give them a solid but cuddly shape, I have stuffed all the woodland animals with uncarded, washed wool fleece. It is ideal for stuffing small toys as it has plenty of bounce, fills the shapes well and reaches right into the tips of small body parts. Some of these wools are naturally brown, which makes them a good choice for filling dark animals.

If you cannot get hold of wool fleece, cotton wool is another good choice, and is readily available and cost-effective. A 100 per cent polyester toy filling could also be used, but it is not as easy to fill small parts with. For this reason, you might want to consider using cotton wool to fill the tips of body parts, then using polyester toy filling to fill the larger parts. Fill the animals a little at a time, teasing the stuffing into place and pushing it right to the tips of the knitted shapes with a chopstick.

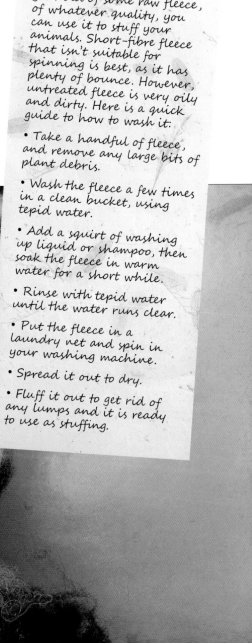

Quick guide to washing raw fleece

If you are lucky enough to get hold of some raw fleece, of whatever quality, you can use it to stuff your animals. Short-fibre fleece that isn't suitable for spinning is best, as it has plenty of bounce. However, untreated fleece is very oily and dirty. Here is a quick guide to how to wash it:

• Take a handful of fleece, and remove any large bits of plant debris.

• Wash the fleece a few times in a clean bucket, using tepid water.

• Add a squirt of washing up liquid or shampoo, then soak the fleece in warm water for a short while.

• Rinse with tepid water until the water runs clear.

• Put the fleece in a laundry net and spin in your washing machine.

• Spread it out to dry.

• Fluff it out to get rid of any lumps and it is ready to use as stuffing.

Needles

Double-pointed needles size 2.75mm (US 2, UK 12)

This is the needle size I used when creating the woodland animals. Your knitting tension needs to be fairly tight, so that when the animals are sewn up the stuffing does not show through between the stitches. If you struggle with knitting DK (8-ply) yarn on such fine needles, experiment with larger needles until you feel more confident. Also remember that synthetic yarn tends to be a bit bulkier than wool types, so this may be another good reason to increase your needle size. I have given a general tension as a guide on page 14, but tensions are not specified for any of the projects in this book, as the size of the finished projects doesn't really matter; you can use the same patterns but different yarns to create very different effects (see page 25). However, if you are making a set of animals, it is a good idea to use the same needle size and yarn weight in order to keep the animals in proportion to each other.

Crochet hook, size 3.00mm (US C/2 or D/3, UK 11)

Projects such as the turtles on pages 78–79 and the top of the tree stump on pages 90–91 are crocheted. The only stitch I've used is double crochet (US single crochet). I have provided some guidance on basic crochet techniques on pages 20–21.

A needle to sew work together

Your animals will be sewn up using the same yarn that you knitted them with – ideally yarn ends if you have left them. I recommend that you use a darning or tapestry needle with a sharp point, as it will be easier to work through your tightly knitted animals than a blunt-ended needle. You can also use the needle for embroidering faces and body parts.

Other tools

Wooden chopsticks

A simple but incredibly effective tool, a chopstick is by far the best instrument for pushing stuffing into your animals. The slender shape is excellent for reaching small, thin animal parts, like legs, but the blunt end won't spoil your stitching. If you don't have any chopsticks, you could use a large knitting needle.

Scissors

Essential for trimming yarn ends when sewing up or creating pompoms. Always keep a small pair of sharp embroidery scissors handy.

Craft pliers

This optional but helpful tool can come in handy when you need to pull out a sewing needle from thick layers of knitted pieces.

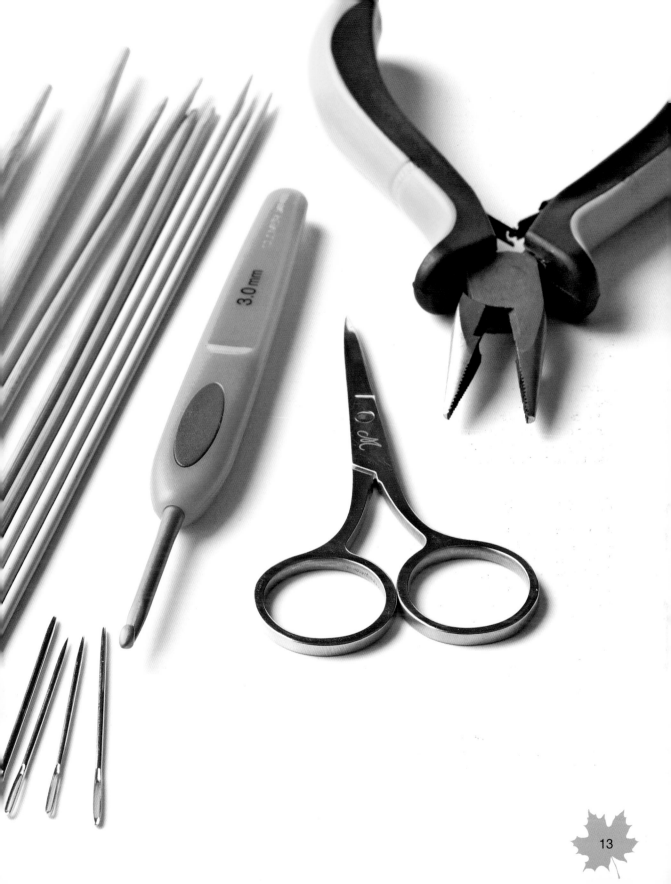

3.0 mm

Basic knitting

The stitches used in this book are just very basic knit and purl. It still amazes me that it is possible to turn small amounts of yarn into something really special using just these two simple techniques. All the animals are knitted flat with two needles.

Increasing and decreasing

To increase one stitch, knit into the front loop and the back loop of the same stitch. This will not create a hole, unlike picking up between the stitches or bringing the yarn forwards. To decrease one stitch, knit or purl two stitches together.

Yarn ends

Always leave long ends when casting on and fastening off for sewing up the piece later. Tuck any unsewn yarn ends inside the body of the animal before you sew it up; not only can you reduce waste in this way, but the colour will match and so the stuffing will be less visible.

Tension (gauge)

This is only a rough guide and it is not essential to follow it, as long as you keep your own tension consistent throughout. I work to a tension of 12 sts and 16 rows over a 4cm (1½in) square, in st/st, using 2.75mm (US 2, UK 12) knitting needles.

Basic crochet

Other than double crochet (US single crochet), I have used only a couple of crochet techniques: making chains and slip stitch.

Tip

Stretch or rest your hands from time to time if you are not used to knitting tight pieces with small needles. Open and close your hands to exercise them and to avoid them becoming stiff.

Abbreviations

Knitting

st/st	stocking stitch (knit on right side rows, purl on wrong side rows)
k	knit
p	purl
inc	increase
dec	decrease
k2tog	knit 2 stitches together
p2tog	purl 2 stitches together
kf/b	knit into front and back of stitch (increasing one stitch)
st(s)	stitch(es)
g-st	garter stitch (knit every row)
pf/b	purl into front and back of stitch (increasing one stitch)
skpo	slip 1, knit 1, pass slipped stitch over
yf	bring yarn forward
yb	bring yarn back
sl1	slip 1 stitch

Crochet

ch	chain
ss	slip stitch: Insert hook into chain and wrap yarn round hook. Draw a new loop through both the chain and the loop on the hook, ending with one loop on the hook
dc	double crochet
sc	single crochet

UK/US crochet abbreviations

Some UK and US crochet terms differ, as shown in the conversion table below. Both UK and US crochet terms have been given throughout this book.

UK		US	
dc	double crochet	sc	single crochet
tr	treble crochet	dc	double crochet

Sewing up and stuffing

The way you sew up your animal will depend on the size. For larger creatures, such as a stag, the legs are created as part of the pattern and are sewn up as shown here. For smaller animals, such as a hare or a squirrel, the legs are created from a simple knitted square as you sew the animal together, see page 19.

The body pieces are tightly knitted, which can sometimes cause the edges to curl up slightly, making them difficult to work with. To create a flat, easy-to-use shape, lay a piece of cloth over the knitted shape and press gently with a steam iron. I have used overcast stitch throughout.

Large animals

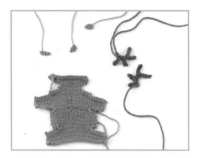

Here are the body, ears, tail and antler pieces needed for the stag. For instructions on how to crochet the antlers, see page 21.

1 Thread a tapestry needle with the yarn at the cast-on end. Starting with a hind leg, fold the leg in half lengthways and close the tip.

2 Using overcast stitch, sew along the first hind leg to the top of the leg.

3 At this point, continue your overcast stitches a little further, attaching one of the flaps on the underside of the body in place, in line with the legs.

4 Join in matching yarn at the tip of the other hind leg and repeat steps 1–3 to sew it up. You do not need to knot the yarn end, simply trap the end inside the leg.

5 Your stag's hind legs should now look like this, with a slight gap between the two pieces on the underside of the body.

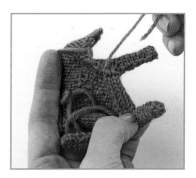

6 Pinch the flaps together on the underside of the body. Using overcast stitch, close the hole between the three edges.

7 Join in new, matching yarn at the tip of one of the front legs and sew along the leg to close it.

8 As in step 3, sew the flap of the underside of the body to the base of the leg.

9 Join in new, matching yarn at the tip of the second front leg and sew along the leg to close it. Also sew the second front flap in place.

10 Using the same piece of yarn, sew from the top of the front legs to the base of the neck.

11 Continue up and over the top of the head. Tuck in any loose yarn ends before completely closing.

12 The stag is now ready for stuffing. Push small pieces of stuffing right into the head and along the legs with a chopstick. Tuck in any remaining yarn ends and fill until the animal feels firm.

13 Join in a strand of new, matching yarn and sew the underside closed, from bottom to top, using overcast stitch.

14 To make the stag look upwards, bring the needle through from the underneath and out at the base of the neck. Work a small neat running stitch down the neck and upper back.

15 Pull the yarn tight to lift the head upwards. You may need to repeat steps 14 and 15 a few times to achieve the right angle. Push the needle back through the body, secure the yarn, and trim.

16 Thread the yarn end of one ear into your needle and sew it to one side of the head. Use a few stitches to secure it, then fasten off and trim the yarn end. Repeat for the other ear.

17 Thread the yarn end of the tail into your needle and sew the tail in place. Use a few stitches to secure it, then fasten off and trim the yarn end.

18 Thread the yarn end of one of the antlers into your needle and sew it in place. Use a few stitches to secure it, then fasten off and trim the yarn end. Repeat for the other antler.

19 To create the eyes, bring a strand of fine yarn (or take two strands from a length of DK / 8-ply yarn) through from the back of the head and out at the front in the position of the first eye, leaving a long tail, then embroider a French knot. Take the needle through the head, bringing it out in the position of the second eye and French knot a second eye.

20 Push the needle out through the back of the head and trim off the end. Thread the yarn ends into the needle then push it back through the neck, through the same hole it came through, to secure the end, then trim it off.

The stag, sewn up and stuffed.

Small animals

Here are the body, ears and head pieces needed for the hare.

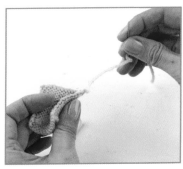

1 Start at one corner of the hare's body piece to create the first hind leg. Thread your needle with the yarn end.

2 Using overcast stitch, sew the two edges together to create a hind leg. Stop when you reach about half way.

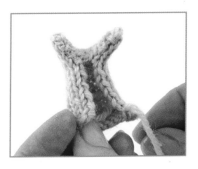

3 Join in a new, matching strand of yarn at the opposite corner and repeat step 2 to create the second hind leg.

4 Create the front two legs as in steps 2 and 3, then stuff the body and legs, using a chopstick to fill right to the ends of the legs. Sew up the body using overcast stitch.

5 Sew across the bottom and side of the folded head piece to create a hollow shape. Tuck in any yarn ends. Push the needle through all the stitches, then pull to tighten.

6 Thread the yarn end of the head piece into your needle and sew in place. Use a few stitches to secure it, then fasten off and trim the yarn end. Repeat to attach both ears.

7 Create a tail by back stitching three times on the same spot. Snip the yarn ends. Embroider French knot eyes and a straight stitch nose using fingering (4-ply) yarn.

The hare, sewn up and stuffed.

Basic crochet

Here are a few basic crochet techniques. You will need to create a starting ring, use double crochet (US single crochet) and close the starting ring, for all the crochet elements in the book.

How to create a starting ring

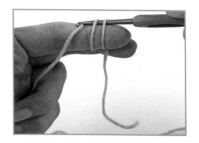  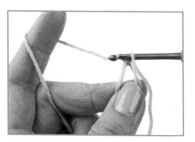

1 Wrap a length of yarn twice around your forefinger and slide the hook through the loops.

2 Use the hook to pull the end of yarn that is connected to the ball of yarn through the loops.

3 Release the ring from your finger and you are ready to begin.

Double crochet (US single crochet)

 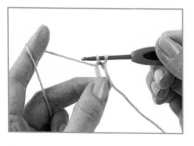 

1 Insert the hook into the ring and wrap the yarn over.

2 Draw the yarn through the ring (two loops on hook).

3 Wrap the yarn over the hook and draw through both loops. You have created 1dc (*US sc*).

Closing the starting ring

1 Once you have completed the required number of stitches, remove the hook from your work, leaving a long loop of yarn. Insert the hook into the ring.

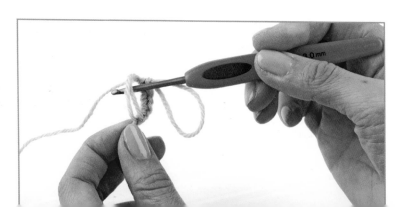

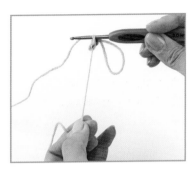

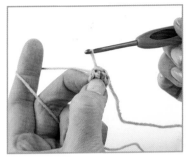

2 Pull the yarn end to tighten the ring around the hook.

3 Insert the hook back into the long loop of yarn you left in step 1, and slip stitch to close the ring.

4 In the next round, work 2dc (*US sc*) into every stitch, to increase. See the pattern on page 94 for further rounds and increases.

Making antlers

The pattern for the stag's antlers is also given on page 48. Once you have mastered the basic technique you can easily adapt it to create antlers of different shapes and sizes, depending on the size of your stag.

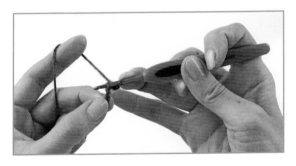

1 With a crochet hook and using dark brown yarn, make 11ch, miss 1ch, ss into the next 5ch.

2 Make 5ch, miss 1ch, ss into the next 4ch.

3 Ss into the next 2ch of the original 11ch, make 4ch, miss 1ch, ss into the next 3ch, ss into the next 2ch of the original 11ch, make 4ch, miss 1ch, ss to the end and fasten off.

4 Thread the yarn through the main part of the antler to strengthen the piece.

Key techniques

How to make an i-cord

I-cords are used for many animal body parts including the turtle's head (see page 78) and the stag's tail (see page 48). Using double-pointed needles, cast on the required number of stitches. Do not turn. Slide stitches to the opposite end of the needle, then knit the stitches again, taking the yarn firmly across the back of the work. Repeat to the desired length. Cast off.

Adding character

The animal patterns in this book are simple, and some are fairly similar to each other. In the beginning, you might think your work doesn't look anything like the animal you are trying to make, but don't despair. You can add a lot of character at the stuffing and embroidery stages and in the positioning of the ears or tail.

Stuffing

When you stuff larger animals, such as foxes, think about how much stuffing you add around the shoulders and back legs, as it can alter the stance. The more you add, the more stocky the animal will look. Add less stuffing around the waist to give the animals a lean, more natural shape. Adding different amounts of stuffing can be a good way to differentiate between males and females.

Embroidery

Study photographs of animals you want to make and note the colour, position and shapes of their facial features. For instance, these cubs have large dark eyes and a long dark line that connects their nose and mouth, creating the impression of a long, broad snout. Foxes, on the other hand, have a longer, more slender snout, with less distance between their nose and mouth, and smaller eyes.

Making pompoms

I've used pompoms to add a bit of extra texture to some of the animals and to make them as lifelike as possible. Mostly the pompoms are used as tails, such as for the wolf, squirrel and skunk (see right), but in the case of the hedgehog, the pompom is the body. Specific instructions are given with each individual pattern.

Making knitted eyes

Most of the animals' eyes are simply French knots, but some, such as those for the owl and the racoon are made in the following way.

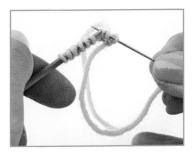

1 Cast on eight stitches. Thread the yarn end into a tapestry needle then transfer the stitches onto the needle.

2 Pull the thread all the way through your eight stitches.

3 Push the needle in through the same end of the stitches and pull through a second time.

4 You should now have created a half-circle shape.

5 Put the needle through the centre of the shape and bring it out at the outer edge.

6 Repeat step 5 to create a circle. Secure in place on your animal with a French knot as a pupil.

Making small body parts with embroidery

Back stitch on the same spot

This is used to make small body parts, such as the hare's tail (see page 70). Thread yarn through the needle. Bring the needle to the front of the work. Insert the needle from front to back and repeat. Work on the same spot so that you can build up small body parts with yarn.

Basic embroidery

Some simple embroidery stitches are used to complete the animals. I most commonly use fingering (4-ply) yarn or two strands taken from DK (8-ply) yarn to embroider faces.

French knots

These are used for most of the animals' eyes. Take the needle through the yarn, separating the fibres, instead of taking the needle out between the stitches. This prevents the eye from sinking into the face.

1 Bring the thread through where the knot is required, at A. Holding the thread between your thumb and finger, wrap it around the needle twice.

2 Hold the thread firmly with your thumb and turn the needle back to A. Insert it as close to A as possible, at B, and pull the thread through to form a knot.

3 Make a small stitch on the wrong side of the fabric before fastening off.

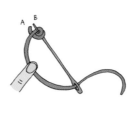

Back stitch

This simple stitch is used to create mouth and nose markings on many of the animals, and colourful back markings on a few others, such as the piglet (page 33) and the fawn (page 50).

1 Bring the needle up at A and pull the thread through. Insert the needle at B and bring it through at C. Pull the thread through the fabric.

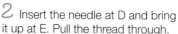

2 Insert the needle at D and bring it up at E. Pull the thread through.

3 Insert the needle at F and bring it up at G. Continue working along the stitch line until it is completed. To finish off, thread your needle through the stitches on the wrong side of your work.

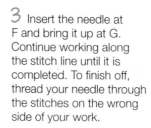

Go wild and use your imagination

You can be innovative when you are knitting this mini woodland scene and try out your own ideas; you do not have to follow all the steps precisely. There's plenty of room for improvisation. Don't be afraid to create the animals and use them in different ways – why not attach a bell and string and make a hanging owl charm, or create a set of small animals, such as the owls and hedgehogs shown below, for a woodland game of noughts and crosses, also known as tick-tack-toe?

These hares were all made using the same pattern; the hare on the left was made with soft fleecy yarn, the centre hare with DK (8-ply) yarn and the hare on the right with mohair yarn.

Making larger or smaller animals

You can make bigger or smaller versions of your animals by using the same pattern but adapting the yarn or needle size, as I did for the hares, shown left. You might also want to try adding fine strands, such as 2-ply or 3-ply yarn, to DK (8-ply) yarn. I sometimes mix my yarns to change the appearance of my animals. If you want to make tiny characters, use 4-ply yarns instead of DK (8-ply) yarn.

25

Making the woodland scene

Brown bear and cubs

Instructions

The body is knitted from the hind legs, finishing at the neck. The head is knitted separately and attached at the end.

Sitting bear

Body and legs

With brown yarn, cast on 25 sts.
Rows 1–6: st/st, starting with a k row.
Row 7: cast off 3 sts, k to end (22).
Row 8: cast off 3 sts, p to end (19).
Row 9: cast on 3 sts, k to end (22).
Row 10: cast on 3 sts, p to end (25).
Rows 11–16: st/st.
Row 17: cast off 3 sts, k to end (22).
Row 18: cast off 3 sts, p to end (19).
Row 19: cast on 3 sts, k these sts, (k5, k2tog) twice, k to end (20).
Row 20: cast on 3 sts, p to end (23).
Rows 21–24: st/st.
Row 25: cast off 3 sts, k to end (20).
Row 26: cast off 3 sts, p to end (17).
Cast off.

Head

With brown yarn, cast on 4 sts, leaving a long end for sewing.

Row 1: p.
Row 2: cast on 3 sts, k to end (7).
Row 3: cast on 3 sts, p to end (10).
Row 4: cast on 2 sts, k to end (12).
Row 5: cast on 2 sts, p to end (14), leave a marking thread at the end of the row.
Row 6: (k3, kf/b) three times, k2 (17).
Rows 7–10: st/st.
Row 11: p2tog to last st, p1 (9).
Rows 12–13: st/st.
Break yarn, leaving a long end, draw through sts, pull tightly and fasten off.

Ears: make two

With brown yarn, cast on 7 sts. Break yarn, draw through sts, pull tightly and fasten off. Following steps 1–4 on page 23, make it into a half circle.

Tail

With brown yarn, cast on 10 sts. Break yarn, draw through sts, pull tightly and fasten off to form a bobble.

Making up

Hind legs: sew each leg from the foot. Sew the under-body flaps along the cast-off edge.
Front legs: sew each leg from the foot. Sew the under-body flaps along the cast-on edge.
Stuff the legs and close the belly.
Head: using the yarn at the fasten-off end, sew up the head just up to

Materials

To make one adult or two cubs:

DK (8-ply) yarn: 10g (1/3oz), brown

Fingering (4-ply) yarn: small amount of black or two strands taken from black DK (8-ply) yarn

Stuffing

Sizes

Adult: 7cm (2¾in) long, 4cm (1½in) high

Cub: 5cm (2in) long, 3cm (1¼in) high

Difficulty level

Intermediate

the marking thread. Stuff the head and attach it to the body using mattress stitch.
Attach the ears and tail.
With black fingering (4-ply) yarn or two strands taken from black DK (8-ply) yarn, embroider a French knot for each eye and create the mouth with back stitch, as shown.

Walking bear

Body, legs, ears and tail

As given for the sitting bear.

Head

Cast on 10 sts with brown yarn and work and make up as given for the sitting bear, omitting rows 2 and 3.

Cub

Body and legs

Cast on 15 sts with brown yarn.
Rows 1–4: st/st, starting with a k row.
Row 5: cast off 2 sts, k to end (13).
Row 6: cast off 2 sts, p to end (11).
Row 7: k, inc 1 st at both ends (13).
Rows 8–11: st/st.
Row 12: p, dec 1 st at both ends (11).
Row 13: cast on 2 sts, k these sts, k4, kf/b, k1, kf/b, k to end (15).
Row 14: cast on 2 sts, p to end (17).
Rows 15–18: st/st.
Cast off.

Head

Cast on 7 sts with brown yarn.
Row 1: p.
Row 2: cast on 3 sts, k to end (10).
Row 3: cast on 3 sts, p to end, leave a marking thread at the end of the row (13).
Rows 4–5: st/st.
Row 6: k1, (k2tog, k1) to end (9).
Rows 7–8: st/st.
Break yarn, draw through sts, pull tightly and fasten off.

Ears: make two

Using brown yarn cast on 3 stitches. Break yarn, draw through sts, pull tightly and fasten off.

Following steps 1–4 on page 23, make it into a half circle.

Tail

Using brown yarn cast on 3 sts. Break yarn, draw through sts, pull tightly and fasten off to form a bobble.

Making up

Follow the instructions given for the sitting bear. The cub's hind legs are on the cast-off end.

Racoon

Instructions

Body, head and legs

With grey yarn, cast on 18 sts.
Rows 1–4: st/st, starting with a
k row.
Row 5: cast off 2 sts, k to end (16).
Row 6: cast off 2 sts, p to end (14).
Row 7: kf/b, k to last st, kf/b (16).
Rows 8–10: st/st.
Row 11: skpo, k to last 2 sts,
k2tog (14).
Row 12: p.
Row 13: cast on 2 sts, k these sts,
k6, (kf/b) twice, k to end (18).
Row 14: cast on 2 sts, p to
end (20).
Row 15: k9, (kf/b) twice, k to
end (22).
Row 16: p.
Row 17: cast off 2 sts, k to end (20).
Row 18: cast off 2 sts, p to
end (18).
Row 19: cast off 3 sts, k to end (15).
Row 20: cast off 3 sts, p to
end (12).
Rows 21–22: st/st.
Row 23: (k1, k2tog) to end (8).
Row 24: p2tog, p4, p2tog (6).
Break yarn, draw through sts, pull
tightly and fasten off.

Tail

Cast on 10 sts with off-white yarn.
Rows 1–3: st/st, starting with a
p row. Do not break yarn.
Rows 4–5: join in dark grey yarn
and st/st. Do not break yarn.
Row 6: with off-white yarn left at
row 3, k2, (k2, k2tog) to end (8).
Row 7: with off-white yarn, p. Do
not break yarn.
Row 8: with dark grey yarn left at

row 5, k1, k2tog, k2, k2tog, k1 (6).
Row 9: with dark grey yarn, p.
Rows 10–11: with off-white yarn
left at row 7, st/st.
Rows 12–13: with dark grey yarn
left at row 9, st/st.
Break yarn, draw through sts, pull
tightly and fasten off.

Ears: make two

With grey yarn, cast on 2 sts and
knit 1 row. Break yarn, slip the
first st over the second st and
fasten off.

Eyes: make two

With two strands taken from
dark grey DK (8-ply) yarn, follow
the steps on page 23 to create
each eye.

Making up

Sew up the body, head and legs
following the basic instructions
on pages 16–18. Attach the ears,
eyes and tail. Embroider a French
knot at the centre of each eye
with white fingering (4-ply) yarn, or
two strands taken from white DK
(8-ply) yarn. Using dark grey DK
(8-ply) yarn, embroider a French
knot for the nose.

Materials

DK (8-ply) yarn: 5g (1/6oz),
grey

DK (8-ply) yarn: small
amounts of off-white
and dark grey

Fingering (4-ply) yarn: small
amount of white or two
strands taken from white
DK (8-ply) yarn

Stuffing

Size

Body: 5cm (2in) long,
3cm (1¼in) high

Tail: 4cm (1½in) long

Difficulty level

Intermediate

Boar and piglets

Instructions

Boar

Body, head and legs

Cast on 18 sts with red-brown yarn.

Rows 1–4: st/st, starting with a k row.

Row 5: cast off 2 sts, k to end (16).

Row 6: cast off 2 sts, p to end (14).

Row 7: cast on 2 sts, k to end (16).

Row 8: cast on 2 sts, p to end (18).

Rows 9–12: st/st.

Row 13: cast off 2 sts, k to end (16).

Row 14: cast off 2 sts, p to end (14).

Row 15: cast on 2 sts, k to end (16).

Row 16: cast on 2 sts, p to end (18).

Rows 17–18: st/st.

Row 19: cast off 2 sts, k5, k2tog, k to end (15).

Row 20: cast off 2 sts, p to end (13).

Row 21: cast off 2 sts, k to end (11).

Row 22: cast off 2 sts, p to end (9).

Row 23: k3, k2tog, k to end (8).

Row 24: p.

Row 25: k3, k2tog, k to end (7).

Row 26: p.

Row 27: k for snout.

Row 28: k.

Break yarn, draw through sts, pull tightly and fasten off.

Ears: make two

Cast on 2 sts with red-brown yarn and purl 1 row, turn. Slip the first st over the second st and fasten off.

Tusks: make two

With white fingering (4-ply) yarn or two strands taken from white DK (8-ply) yarn, cast on 3 sts and st/st 3 rows. Break yarn, draw through sts and fasten off.

Tail

Make 5 chains with a crochet hook and red-brown yarn. Fasten off. Hide the fasten-off yarn end inside the tail.

Making up

Sew up the body, head and legs and stuff. For the tusks, sew the side edges starting at the fasten-off end and pull the yarn to shape. Attach ears, tusks and tail. Embroider a French knot for each eye using black fingering (4-ply) yarn or two strands taken from DK (8-ply) yarn.

Materials

To make one boar:

DK (8-ply): 4g ($\frac{1}{8}$oz), red-brown

Fingering (4-ply) yarn: small amount of white or two strands taken from white DK (8-ply) yarn

Fingering (4-ply) yarn: small amount of black or two strands taken from black DK (8-ply) yarn

Stuffing

To make one piglet:

DK (8-ply) yarn: small amounts of light brown and beige or off-white

Fingering (4-ply) yarn: small amount of black or two strands taken from black DK (8-ply) yarn

Stuffing

Additional equipment

3mm (US C/2 or D/3, UK 11) crochet hook

Sizes

Boar: 6cm (2½in) long, 3cm (1¼in) high

Piglet: 5cm (2in) long, 2.5cm (1in) high

Difficulty level

Intermediate

Piglet

Body, head and legs

Cast on 14 sts with light brown yarn.

Rows 1–4: st/st, starting with a
k row.

Row 5: cast off 2 sts, k to end (12).

Row 6: cast off 2 sts, p to end (10).

Row 7: cast on 2 sts, k to end (12).

Row 8: cast on 2 sts, p to end (14).

Rows 9–10: st/st.

Row 11: cast off 2 sts, k to end (12).

Row 12: cast off 2 sts, p to end (10).

Row 13: cast on 2 sts, k to end (12).

Row 14: cast on 2 sts, p to end (14).

Rows 15–16: st/st.

Row 17: cast off 3 sts, k to end (11).

Row 18: cast off 3 sts, p to end (8).

Row 19: k3, k2tog, k to end (7).

Row 20: p.

Row 21: k2, k2tog, k to end (6).

Row 22: p.

Row 23: (k2, k2tog) to end (4).

Row 24: k for snout.

Row 25: k.

Break yarn, draw through sts, pull
tightly and fasten off.

Ears: make two

As given for the boar but use two
strands of light brown DK (8-ply)
yarn. Alternatively, back stitch on the
same spot three times.

Tail

Make 4 chains with a crochet hook
and light brown yarn. Fasten off.
Hide the fasten-off yarn end inside
the tail.

Making up

Follow the instructions given for the
boar. Embroider the stripes with
back stitch, using beige or
off-white DK (8-ply) yarn. Embroider
a French knot for each eye using
black fingering (4-ply) yarn or two
strands taken from DK (8-ply) yarn.

Badger

Instructions

Body, head and legs

With dark grey yarn, cast on 18 sts.

Rows 1–4: st/st, starting with a k row.

Row 5: cast off 2 sts, k to end (16).

Row 6: cast off 2 sts, p to end (14).

Row 7: cast on 2 sts, k to end (16).

Row 8: cast on 2 sts, p to end (18).

Rows 9–12: st/st.

Row 13: cast off 2 sts, k to end (16).

Row 14: cast off 2 sts, p to end (14).

Row 15: cast on 2 sts, k to end (16).

Row 16: cast on 2 sts, p to end (18).

Rows 17–18: st/st.

Row 19: cast off 2 sts, k to end (16).

Row 20: cast off 2 sts, p to end (14).

Row 21: k1, k2tog, k3, k2tog, k3, k2tog, k1 (11).

Row 22: p.

Row 23: join in white yarn. K3 (white), k1 (dark grey), k3 (white), k1 (dark grey), k3 (white).

Row 24: p3 (white), p1 (dark grey), p2tog, p1 (white), p1 (dark grey), p3 (white) (10).

Row 25: keeping the colours correct, k.

Row 26: keeping the colours correct, p.

Row 27: k1, k2tog (white), k1 (dark grey), k2tog (white), k1 (dark grey), k2tog, k1 (white) (7).

Row 28: keeping the colours correct, p.

Break yarn, draw through sts, pull tightly and fasten off.

Tail

Cast on 4 sts with dark grey or black yarn.

Rows 1–3: st/st, starting with a p row.

Row 4: k1, k2tog, k1 (3).

Break yarn, draw through sts, pull tightly and fasten off.

Ears: make two

Separate out two strands from a length of dark grey DK (8-ply) yarn. Cast on 2 sts, purl 1 row, turn. Slip the first st over the second st and fasten off.

Making up

Sew the body, head and legs following the basic instructions. Attach the ears and sew up and attach the tail. Embroider a French knot for each eye using black fingering (4-ply) yarn or two strands taken from DK (8-ply) yarn.

Materials

DK (8-ply) yarn: 5g (¹⁄₆oz), dark grey

DK (8-ply) yarn: small amount of white

Fingering (4-ply) yarn: a small amount of black or two strands taken from black DK (8-ply) yarn

Stuffing

Size

7cm (2¾in) long, 3cm (1¼in) high

Difficulty level

Beginner

Beaver

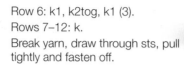

Instructions

Body and head

With dark brown yarn, cast on 9 sts loosely.
Row 1: kf/b in every st (18).
Rows 2–8: st/st, starting with a p row.
Row 9: k2, (k2tog, k2) to end (14).
Row 10: p.
Row 11: k2, (k2tog, k2) to end (11).
Row 12: p.
Row 13: k2, (kf/b, k2) to end (14).
Row 14: p.
Row 15: k.
Row 16: (p1, p2tog) to last 2 sts, p2 (10).
Row 17: k2tog to end (5).
Break yarn, draw through sts, pull tightly and fasten off.

Feet: make two

Cast on 3 sts with dark brown yarn.
Rows 1–6: st/st, starting with a p row.
Row 7: k for fold line.
Rows 8–13: st/st, starting with a k row.
Cast off.

Arms: make two

With dark brown yarn, cast on 2 sts and work an i-cord (see page 22) for 3 rows. Fasten off.

Tail

Worked in garter stitch. With grey yarn, cast on 4 sts.
Rows 1–5: k.

Row 6: k1, k2tog, k1 (3).
Rows 7–12: k.
Break yarn, draw through sts, pull tightly and fasten off.

Making up

Sew the body and head and stuff. The seam will be on the tummy. Fold each foot in half at the folding line and sew all the sides. Attach them to the base of the body. Attach arms and tail. Create ears by back stitching on the same spot several times with dark brown DK (8-ply) yarn. Using small, straight stitches, embroider the eyes, nose and mouth with black fingering (4-ply) yarn or two strands taken from black DK (8-ply) yarn. Embroider two straight, vertical stitches for the teeth using white fingering (4-ply) yarn or two strands taken from white DK (8-ply) yarn, as shown.

Materials

DK (8-ply) yarn: small amounts of dark brown and grey

Fingering (4-ply) yarn: small amounts of black and white

Stuffing

Size

If the feet are attached underneath, the beaver will measure: 5.5cm (2¼in) high and 5.5cm (2¼in) long, including the tail

If the feet are attached to the tummy, the beaver will measure: 5cm (2in) high and 7cm (2¾in) long, including the tail

Difficulty level

Beginner

Variation

Attach the feet to the tummy.

Skunk

Instructions

Body, head and legs

Starting with the hind legs, cast on 18 sts in dark grey yarn.

Row 1: p.

Row 2: k6 (dark grey), join in white yarn, k2 (white), k2 (dark grey), k2 (white), k6 (dark grey).

Rows 3–4: keeping the colours correct, st/st.

Row 5: cast off 2 sts, p to end with colour pattern (16).

Row 6: keeping the colour correct, cast off 2 sts, k to end (14).

Row 7: keeping the colour correct, p, inc 1 st at both ends (16).

Rows 8–10: st/st with colour pattern.

Row 11: keeping the colour correct, p, dec 1 st at both ends (14).

Row 12: keeping the colour correct, k.

Row 13: cast on 2 sts with dark grey, keeping the colour correct, p to end (16).

Row 14: cast on 2 sts with dark grey, k these sts, k4 (dark grey), k2 (white), (kf/b) twice (white), k2 (white), k to end (dark grey) (20).

Rows 15–16: keeping the colour correct, st/st.

Row 17: cast off 2 sts, p3 (dark grey), p6 (white), p to end (dark grey) (18).

Row 18: cast off 2 sts, k3 (dark grey), k4 (white), k to end (dark grey) (16).

Row 19: cast off 3 sts, p3 (dark grey), p2 (white), p to end (dark grey) (13).

Row 20: cast off 3 sts, k to end with dark grey. Break off white yarn (10).

Row 21: p1, (p2tog, p1) to end (7).

Row 22: k.

Row 23: p2tog, p3, p2tog (5).

Break yarn, draw through sts, pull tightly and fasten off.

Ears: make two

With two strands taken from dark grey DK (8-ply) yarn, cast on 2 sts, purl 1 row, turn. Slip the first st over the second st and fasten off.

Tail

Cut a piece of card 2 x 5cm (¾ x 2in). Wind white yarn around it about fifteen times to form one layer, then wind dark grey yarn over the white another fifteen times. Sew up the centre of the piece of card using small running stitches, securing the thread at each end, then cut and release the card.

Making up

Sew each leg, then sew the head from the tip of the nose to the centre of the body. Stuff the body, head and legs and close the seam. Attach the ears and the tail. Embroider a French knot for each eye using white fingering (4-ply) yarn or two strands taken from DK (8-ply) yarn.

Materials

DK (8-ply) yarn: 4g (⅛oz), dark grey

DK (8-ply) yarn: 4g (⅛oz), white

Stuffing

Strong cotton thread for making pompom

Size

5cm (2in) high including tail, 7cm (2¾in) long

Difficulty level

Intermediate

Fox

Instructions

Body, head and legs

Cast on 18 sts with light brown yarn.

Rows 1–5: st/st, starting with a k row.

Row 6: cast off 3 sts, p to end (15).

Row 7: cast off 3 sts, k to end (12).

Row 8: cast on 2 sts, p to end (14).

Row 9: cast on 2 sts, k to end (16).

Rows 10–15: st/st.

Row 16: cast off 2 sts, p to end (14).

Row 17: cast off 2 sts, k to end (12).

Row 18: cast on 3 sts, p to end (15).

Row 19: cast on 3 sts, k these sts, k5, (kf/b) twice, k to end (20).

Row 20: p.

Row 21: k9, (kf/b) twice, k to end (22).

Row 22: p.

Row 23: k10, (kf/b) twice, k to end (24).

Row 24: cast off 3 sts, p to end (21).

Row 25: cast off 3 sts, k to last st, join in white yarn and k the last st with white (18).

Row 26: cast off 4 sts with white, p to last st with light brown, join in white yarn and p the last st with white (14).

Row 27: cast off 4 sts with white, k to last st with light brown, k the last st with white (10).

Row 28: pf/b (white), p to last st (light brown), pf/b (white) (12).

Row 29: keeping the colours correct, k.

Row 30: keeping the colours correct, p.

Row 31: break off light brown yarn, k all sts with white yarn.

Row 32: (p2tog) to end (6).

Row 33: k.

Row 34: (p2tog) to end (3).

Break yarn, draw through sts, pull tightly and fasten off.

Ears: make two

Cast on 3 sts with light brown yarn.

Rows 1–2: st/st, starting with a p row.

Row 3: p1, p2tog (2).

Row 4: k2tog (1).

Fasten off.

Tail

Cast on 8 sts with light brown yarn.

Rows 1–4: st/st, starting with a k row.

Row 5: k1, k2tog, k2, k2tog, k1 (6).

Row 6: change to white yarn and p.

Row 7: k.

Row 8: (p2tog) to end (3).

Break yarn, draw through sts, pull tightly and fasten off.

Making up

Sew the body, head and legs following the basic sewing instructions (see pages 16–18).

(see pages 16–18)

Materials

DK (8-ply) yarn: 5g (1/6oz), light brown

DK (8-ply) yarn: small amount of white

Fingering (4-ply) yarn: small amount of dark brown or two strands taken from dark brown DK (8-ply) yarn

Stuffing

Size

Body: 7cm (2¾in) long, 3cm (1¼in) high

Tail: 2cm (¾in) long

Difficulty level

Beginner

Attach the ears. Sew the tail seam and stuff, then attach to the body. Work a gathering thread around the neck line and pull tightly to shape. Embroider the eyes, nose and mouth with dark brown fingering (4-ply) yarn or two strands taken from dark brown DK (8-ply) yarn; sew French knots for the eyes, and create the nose and mouth using small, straight back stitches, as shown.

Otter

Instructions

Otter on all fours

Body, head and tail

The body is knitted from the tail to the head.

Cast on 3 sts with dark brown yarn.

Row 1: k.
Row 2: p.
Row 3: k1, kf/b, k1 (4).
Row 4: p.
Row 5: k1, (kf/b) twice, k1 (6).
Rows 6–8: st/st.
Row 9: (k1, kf/b) to end (9).
Rows 10–12: st/st.
Row 13: k1, (kf/b, k2) twice, kf/b, k1 (12).
Row 14: p.
Row 15: cast on 2 sts, k to end (14).
Row 16: cast on 2 sts, p to end (16).
Rows 17–22: st/st.
Row 23: shape front legs; cast on 2 sts, k to end (18).
Row 24: cast on 2 sts, p to end (20).
Row 25: k9, (kf/b) twice, k to end (22).
Row 26: p.
Row 27: cast off 2 sts, k to end (20).
Row 28: cast off 2 sts, p to end (18).
Row 29: cast off 3 sts, k to end (15).
Row 30: cast off 3 sts, p to end (12).
Row 31: k2tog, k3, (kf/b) twice, k3, k2tog (12).
Rows 32–34: st/st.

Row 35: k2tog, k to last st, k2tog (10).
Rows 36–37: st/st.
Row 38: p1, (p2tog, p1) to end (7).
Break yarn, draw through sts, pull tightly and fasten off.

Hind legs: make two

Cast on 3 sts with dark brown yarn.
Rows 1–6: st/st, starting with a p row.
Row 7: k for fold line.
Rows 8–13: st/st, starting with a k row.
Cast off.

Front feet: make two

Cast on 3 sts with dark brown yarn.
Row 1: p.
Row 2: k.
Row 3: p1, p2tog (2).
Cast off.

Making up

Using the yarn at the fasten-off end, sew the body seam up to the front legs. Sew each front leg. Using the yarn at the cast-on end, sew the body up to the tummy. Stuff and close the seam. The hind legs do not need stuffing – fold each piece in half at the folding line and sew the pieces together before attaching. Attach front feet to the base of each front leg. Create ears by back stitching on the same spot three times with dark brown DK (8-ply) yarn. Embroider the eyes and nose using black fingering (4-ply) yarn or two strands taken from black DK (8-ply) yarn – embroider a French knot for each eye, and create the nose using small, straight stitches. Embroider the whiskers with light brown fingering (4-ply) yarn or two strands taken from light brown DK (8-ply) yarn – create small, straight stitches across the cheeks, as shown.

Materials

Each otter:

DK (8-ply) yarn: 4g (¹⁄₈oz), dark brown

Fingering (4-ply) yarn: small amounts of black and light brown or two strands taken from black and light brown DK (8-ply) yarn

Stuffing

Sizes

Otter on all fours: 9cm (3½in) long, 4cm (1½in) high

Upright otter: 6cm (2½in) high, 4cm (1½in) long

Difficulty level

Beginner

Upright otter

Body, head and tail

Knit the body following the pattern for the otter on all fours until row 22.

Row 23: k.

Row 24: p.

Row 25: k7, (kf/b) twice, k to end (18).

Row 26: p.

Row 27: k.

Row 28: p.

Row 29: cast off 3 sts, k to end (15).

Row 30: cast off 3 sts, p to end (12).

Row 31: k2tog, k3, (kf/b) twice, k3, k2tog (12).

Rows 32–34: st/st.

Row 35: k2tog, k to last 2 sts, k2tog (10).

Rows 36–37: st/st.

Row 38: p1, (p2tog, p1) to end (7). Break yarn, draw through sts, pull tightly and fasten off.

Hind legs: make two

Follow the instructions given for the otter on all fours.

Front legs: make two

Cast on 2 sts with dark brown yarn and work as an i-cord (see page 22) for 4 rows. Fasten off.

Making up

Follow the instructions given for the otter on all fours. Attach the front legs to the top front of the otter's body.

Wolf

Instructions

Body, head and legs

Cast on 20 sts with dark grey yarn.

Rows 1–5: st/st, starting with a k row.

Row 6: cast off 4 sts, p to end (16).

Row 7: cast off 4 sts, k to end (12).

Row 8: cast on 2 sts, p to end (14).

Row 9: cast on 2 sts, k to end (16).

Rows 10–15: st/st.

Row 16: cast off 2 sts, p to end (14).

Row 17: cast off 2 sts, k to end (12).

Row 18: cast on 4 sts, p to end (16).

Row 19: cast on 4 sts, k5, (kf/b) twice, k to end (22).

Row 20: p.

Row 21: k10, (kf/b) twice, k to end (24).

Row 22: p.

Row 23: k11, (kf/b) twice, k to end (26).

Row 24: cast off 4 sts, p to end (22).

Row 25: cast off 4 sts, k to end (18).

Row 26: cast off 4 sts, p to end (14).

Row 27: cast off 4 sts, k to end (10).

Row 28: cast on 3 sts, p to end (13).

Row 29: cast on 3 sts, k to end (16).

Rows 30–31: st/st.

Row 32: p2tog, cast off the st on the right hand needle, cast off all the sts until the last 2 sts, p2tog, pass the first st over the second st and fasten off.

Ears: make two

Cast on 2 sts with dark grey yarn and purl 1 row, turn. Slip the first st over the second st and fasten off.

Tail

Wind dark grey DK (8-ply) yarn around two of your fingers 25 times, then tie between your fingers with strong cotton thread. Release from your fingers and cut the loops to shape an oblong about 2cm (¾in) long.

Making up

Sew the body, head and legs following the basic sewing instructions on pages 16–18. Attach ears and tail. Embroider each eye with a French knot or small back stitches using white fingering (4-ply) yarn or two strands taken from white DK (8-ply) yarn. Pull the yarn to make a slight dent if desired. Embroider the nose with small straight stitches, using black fingering (4-ply) yarn or two strands taken from black DK (8-ply) yarn.

Materials

DK (8-ply) yarn: 8g (¼oz), dark grey

Fingering (4-ply) yarn: small amounts of white and black or two strands taken from white and black DK (8-ply) yarn

Stuffing

Strong cotton thread for making pompom

Size

7cm (2¾in) long, 5cm (2in) high

Difficulty level

Beginner

Moose

Instructions

Body, head and legs

Cast on 25 sts with dark brown yarn.

Rows 1–6: st/st, starting with a k row.

Row 7: cast off 6 sts, k to end (19).

Row 8: cast off 6 sts, p to end (13).

Row 9: cast on 3 sts, k to end (16).

Row 10: cast on 3 sts, p to end (19).

Rows 11–18: st/st.

Row 19: cast off 3 sts, k to end (16).

Row 20: cast off 3 sts, p to end (13).

Row 21: cast on 6 sts, k5, kf/b, k1, kf/b, k to end (21).

Row 22: cast on 6 sts, p to end (27).

Row 23: k4, kf/b, k7, kf/b, k1, kf/b, k7, kf/b, k4 (31).

Row 24: p.

Rows 25–28: st/st.

Row 29: cast off 6 sts, k to end (25).

Row 30: cast off 6 sts, p to end (19).

Row 31: cast off 4 sts, k to end (15).

Row 32: cast off 4 sts, p to end (11).

Row 33: cast on 4 sts, k to end (15).

Row 34: cast on 4 sts, p to end (19).

Rows 35–37: st/st.

Row 38: p2tog, cast off the stitch on the right needle cast off all the stitches until the last 2 stitches, p2tog, pass the first st over the second st and fasten off.

Ears: make two

Cast on 2 sts with dark brown yarn, purl 1 row, turn. Pass the first st over the second st and fasten off.

Tail

Work a 2-stitch i-cord (see page 22) for 1cm (½in) with dark brown yarn. Break yarn, draw through sts, pull tightly and fasten off.

Bell

Cast on 4 sts with dark brown yarn.

Row 1: k.

Row 2: k1, k2tog, k1 (3).

Row 3: k1, k2tog (2).

Pass the first st over the second st and fasten off.

Antlers: make two

With a crochet hook and brown DK (8-ply) yarn make 14ch (base chains). Miss 1ch, ss to next 6ch, make 5ch, miss 1ch, ss in next 4ch, 1 ss in base chain, * make 4ch, miss 1ch, ss in next 3ch, 1ss to base ch, repeat from * 4 more times and fasten off leaving a long end. Take the fasten-off end of the yarn through the entire width of the antler piece to secure and connect the antlers' points.

Making up

Sew the body following the basic sewing instructions on pages 16–18. Attach ears, tail, bell and antlers. Embroider a French knot for each eye with black fingering (4-ply) yarn or two strands taken from black DK (8-ply) yarn.

Stag and doe

Instructions

Stag

Body, head and legs

Cast on 24 sts with red-brown yarn.

Rows 1–6: st/st, starting with a k row.

Row 7: cast off 6 sts, k to end (18).

Row 8: cast off 6 sts, p to end (12).

Row 9: cast on 3 sts, k to end (15).

Row 10: cast on 3 sts, p to end (18).

Rows 11–16: st/st.

Row 17: cast off 3 sts, k to end (15).

Row 18: cast off 3 sts, p to end (12).

Row 19: cast on 6 sts, k these sts, k5, (kf/b) twice, k to end (20).

Row 20: cast on 6 sts, p to end (26).

Row 21: k12, (kf/b) twice, k to end (28).

Row 22: p.

Row 23: k13, (kf/b) twice, k to end (30).

Row 24: p.

Row 25: cast off 6 sts, k to end (24).

Row 26: cast off 6 sts, p to end (18).

Row 27: cast off 4 sts, k to end (14).

Row 28: cast off 4 sts, p to end (10).

Row 29: k.

Row 30: p2tog, p to last 2 sts, p2tog (8).

Row 31: cast on 3 sts, k to end (11).

Row 32: cast on 3 sts, p to end (14).

Row 33: k, inc 1 st at both ends (16).

Row 34: p.

Row 35: k2tog, cast off the stitch on the right hand needle, cast off all the sts until the last 2 sts, k2tog. Pass the first st over the second st and fasten off.

Ears: make two

Cast on 3 sts with red-brown yarn.

Row 1: p.

Row 2: k.

Row 3: p2tog, p1 (2).

Pass the first st over the second st and fasten off.

Tail

Work a 2-stitch i-cord (see page 22) with red-brown yarn for 3 rows.

Antlers: make two

With a crochet hook using dark brown DK (8-ply) yarn, make 11ch, miss 1ch, ss to next 5ch, make 5ch, miss 1ch, ss to next 4ch, ss to next 2ch on the first 11ch, make 4ch, miss 1ch, ss to next 3ch, ss to next 2ch on the first 11ch, make 4ch, miss 1ch, ss to the end and fasten off.

Thread the yarn through the main part of the antler to strengthen the piece. See also the instructions on page 21.

Making up

Follow the basic instructions on pages 16–18. Sew up the body, head and legs, then work a gathering thread through the back of the neck to keep the head up and create a curved neck. Attach ears, tail and antlers. Embroider a French knot for each eye with dark

Materials

DK (8-ply) yarn: 7g (¼oz), red-brown

DK (8-ply) yarn: small amount of dark brown

Fingering (4-ply) yarn: small amount of dark brown or two strands taken from dark brown DK (8-ply) yarn

Additional equipment

3mm (US C/2 or D/3, UK 11) crochet hook

Size

Body: 8cm (3in) long, 6cm (2½in) high

Antlers: 2.5cm (1in) high

Difficulty level

Intermediate

brown fingering (4-ply) yarn or two strands taken from dark brown DK (8-ply) yarn. Use the same yarn to sew the nose – back stitch a few times in the same place to create it.

Doe

Follow the pattern given for the stag but omit the antlers.

Fawn

Instructions

Body, head and legs

Cast on 20 sts with light brown yarn.

Rows 1–5: st/st, starting with a k row.

Row 6: cast off 4 sts, p to end (16).

Row 7: cast off 4 sts, k to end (12).

Row 8: cast on 2 sts, p to end (14).

Row 9: cast on 2 sts, k to end (16).

Rows 10–15: st/st.

Row 16: cast off 2 sts, p to end (14).

Row 17: cast off 2 sts, k to end (12).

Row 18: cast on 4 sts, p to end (16).

Row 19: cast on 4 sts, k these sts, k5, (kf/b) twice, k to end (22).

Row 20: p.

Row 21: k10, (kf/b) twice, k to end (24).

Row 22: p.

Row 23: k11, (kf/b) twice, k to end (26).

Row 24: cast off 4 sts, p to end (22).

Row 25: cast off 4 sts, k to end (18).

Row 26: cast off 5 sts, p to end (13).

Row 27: cast off 5 sts, k to end (8).

Row 28: cast on 3 sts, p to end (11).

Row 29: cast on 3 sts, k to end (14).

Rows 30–31: st/st.

Row 32: p2tog, cast off the st on the right hand needle, cast off all the sts until the last 2 sts, p2tog. Pass the first st over the second st and fasten off.

Ears: make two

Follow the instructions given for the stag (see page 48), but with light brown yarn.

Tail

Work a 2-stitch i-cord (see page 22) with light brown yarn for 3 rows. Break yarn, draw through sts, pull tightly and fasten off.

Making up

Follow the instructions given for the stag and doe on page 48. Using dark brown fingering (4-ply) yarn or two strands taken from dark brown DK (8-ply) yarn, embroider a French knot for each eye and sew a few back stitches to create the nose. Embroider back stitch stripes along the fawn's back using white DK (8-ply) yarn and add French knot dots with red-brown DK (8-ply) yarn if desired, as shown.

Materials

DK (8-ply) yarn: 7g (¼oz), light brown

DK (8-ply) yarn: small amounts of white and red-brown

Fingering (4-ply) yarn: small amount of dark brown or two strands taken from dark brown DK (8-ply) yarn

Stuffing

Size

7cm (2¾in) long, 5cm (2in) high

Difficulty level

Intermediate

Duck

Instructions

Male

Body, head and tail

Starting with the tail, cast on 7 sts with light brown or grey yarn.
Row 1: p.
Row 2: k2, kf/b, k1, kf/b, k2 (9).
Row 3: p.
Row 4: k3, (kf/b) three times, k3 (12).
Row 5: p.
Row 6: k.
Row 7: p.
Row 8: k3, (k2tog) three times, k3 (9).
Row 9: change to brown yarn and p.
Row 10: k6, yf, sl1, yb, turn.
Row 11: sl1, p3, yb, sl1, yf, turn.
Row 12: sl1, k3, yf, sl1, yb, turn.
Row 13: sl1, p2, yb, sl1, yf, turn.
Row 14: sl1, k to end.
Row 15: (p2tog) four times, p1 (5).
Row 16: change to green yarn and k.
Row 17: p.
Row 18: k1, kf/b, k1, kf/b, k1 (7).
Row 19: p.
Row 20: k.
Row 21: (p2tog) three times, p1 (4).
Break yarn, draw through sts, pull tightly and fasten off.

Wings: make two

Cast on 6 sts with light brown or grey yarn.
Rows 1–3: st/st, starting with a p row.
Row 4: (k1, k2tog) to end (4).
Row 5: p.
Break yarn, draw through sts, pull tightly and fasten off.

Beak

Cast on 3 sts with yellow yarn.
P2tog, p1, turn. Slip the first st over the second st and fasten off. Hide the fasten-off end of the yarn inside the beak.

Making up

Sew the body seam from both the fasten-off end and from the cast-on end, leaving a small opening in the middle for stuffing. Stuff the body and head and close the seam. Squash down the neck and secure the head with a few stitches. The seam will be on the top of the body. You will need to sew up the wings before you attach them. Also attach the beak. Embroider a French knot for each eye with dark brown fingering (4-ply) yarn or two strands taken from dark brown DK (8-ply) yarn.

Female

Knit the body and head with light brown yarn only, following the instructions given for the male duck. Knit the wings with light brown and dark brown yarn mix or take two strands from each of dark and light brown DK (8-ply) yarns and knit them together.

Making up

Follow the instructions given for the male duck.

Variation

Use white yarn to create a white duck.

Materials

For male:

DK (8-ply) yarn: small amounts of green, light brown, grey, brown and yellow

Fingering (4-ply) yarn: small amount of dark brown or two strands taken from dark brown DK (8-ply) yarn

Stuffing

For female:

DK (8-ply) yarn: small amounts of light brown, yellow and light and dark brown mix

Fingering (4-ply) yarn: small amount of dark brown or two strands taken from dark brown DK (8-ply yarn)

Stuffing

Size

4cm (1½in) long, 2cm (¾in) high

Difficulty level

Intermediate

Swan and cygnets

Instructions

Swan

Body, head and tail

Starting with the tail, cast on 8 sts with white yarn.

Row 1: p.
Row 2: k2, (kf/b, k2) to end (10).
Row 3: p.
Row 4: k3, (kf/b) four times, k3 (14).
Rows 5–9: st/st.
Row 10: k2, (k2tog, k2) to end (11).
Row 11: p.
Row 12: k7, yf, sl1, yb, turn.
Row 13: sl1, p3, yb, sl1, yf, turn.
Row 14: sl1, k3, yf, sl1, yb, turn.
Row 15: sl1, p3, yb, sl1, yf turn.
Row 16: sl1, k to end.
Row 17: (p2tog) five times, p1 (6).
Rows 18–23: st/st.
Row 24: k1, kf/b, k2, kf/b, k1 (8).
Row 25: p2 (white), add in black yarn, p4 (black), p2 (white).
Row 26: break off white yarn, k with black yarn only.
Row 27: (p2tog) to end (4).
Break yarn, draw through sts, pull tightly and fasten off.

Beak

With yellow yarn, cast on 3 sts, p2tog, p1, turn.
Slip the first st over the second st and fasten off. Hide the fasten-off end of the yarn inside the beak.

Wings: make two

Cast on 10 sts with white yarn.
Rows 1–3: st/st, starting with a p row.
Row 4: k1, (k2tog, k1) to end (7).
Row 5: p.
Row 6: k1, (k2tog, k1) to end (5).
Row 7: p.
Row 8: k1, k2tog, k2 (4).
Row 9: p.
Break yarn, draw through sts, pull tightly and fasten off.

Cygnet

Body, head and tail

Starting with the tail, cast on 4 sts with grey yarn.
Row 1: k1, (kf/b) twice, k1 (6).
Row 2: p.
Row 3: (k1, kf/b, k1) twice (8).
Row 4: p.
Row 5: k5, yf, sl1, yb, turn.
Row 6: sl1, p2, yb, sl1, yf, turn.
Row 7: sl1, k to end.
Row 8: p.
Row 9: k.
Row 10: p2tog, (p1, p2tog) to end (5).
Row 11: k1, (kf/b, k1) twice (7).
Break yarn, draw through sts, pull tightly and fasten off.

Wings: make two

Cast on 3 sts with grey yarn.
Row 1: p.

Materials

DK (8-ply) yarn: small amounts of white, black, grey and yellow

Fingering (4-ply) yarn: small amount of dark brown or two strands taken from dark brown DK (8-ply) yarn

Stuffing

Size

Swan: 5cm (2in) long, 3cm (1¼in) high

Cygnet: 2.5cm (1in) long, 2cm (¾in) high

Difficulty level

Intermediate

Row 2: k.
Row 3: p2tog, p1 (2).
Row 4: skpo and fasten off.

Making up

Sew the body and head from both the cast-on end and the fasten-off end, leaving a small opening. Stuff the body and head and close the seam. You will need to sew up the wings before you attach them. Also attach the beak. For the cygnet, create a beak by back stitching on the same spot a few times with two strands taken from yellow DK (8-ply) yarn. Embroider a French knot for each eye with dark brown fingering (4-ply) yarn or two strands taken from dark brown DK (8-ply) yarn.

Peacock

Instructions

Body and head

Starting with the base, cast on 6 sts with blue yarn.
Row 1: kf/b in every st (12).
Row 2: k for fold line.
Rows 3–10: st/st, starting with a k row.
Row 11: (k1, k2tog) to end (8).
Rows 12–14: st/st.
Row 15: k2tog, (k1, k2tog) to end (5).
Break yarn, draw through sts, pull tightly and fasten off.

Tail

Cast on 46 sts with blue-green yarn.
Row 1: k2, (p2, k2) to end.
Row 2: p2, (k2, p2) to end.
Row 3: k2, (p2, k2) to end.
Row 4: change to light green yarn, p2, (k2, p2) to end.
Row 5: k2, (p2, k2) to end.
Row 6: p2, (k2, p2) to end.
Row 7: change to green yarn, k2, (p2tog, k2) to end (35).
Row 8: p2, (k1, p2) to end.
Row 9: k2, (p1, k2) to end.
Row 10: p2tog, (k1, p2tog) to end (23).
Row 11: k1, (p1, k1) to end.
Row 12: change to light green yarn, p1, (k1, p1) to end.
Row 13: k1, (p1, k1) to end.
Row 14: change to green yarn, p1 (k1, p1) to end.
Row 15: k1 (p1, k1) to end.
Row 16: (p1, k2tog) to last 2 sts, p2tog (15).

Row 17: k1, (p1, k1) to end.
Row 18: p1, (k1, p1) to end.
Row 19: k1, (p1, k1) to end.
Break yarn, draw through sts, pull tightly and fasten off.

Making up

Sew the body and head from the fasten-off end. Insert a ceramic baking bean, add a little stuffing to the body and head and close the seam. The seam will be on back side of the head and body. With yellow DK (8-ply) yarn, create the beak by back stitching on the same spot three times. Embroider the feet: sew three small straight stitches for each foot at the base of the body, using yellow DK (8-ply) yarn. With dark brown fingering (4-ply) yarn, or two strands taken from dark brown DK (8-ply) yarn, back stitch three loose loops on top of the head and work a French knot for each eye. Attach the tail to the lower back of the body.

Variation

Fold the tail back after attaching it to the lower back of the body.

Eagle

Instructions

Body and head

Starting with the base, cast on 6 sts with black yarn.

Row 1: kf/b in every st (12).

Row 2: p.

Row 3: (k1, kf/b) to end (18).

Row 4: k for fold line.

Rows 5–6: st/st, starting with a k row.

Row 7: k2tog, k to last 2 sts, k2tog (16).

Rows 8–12: st/st, starting with a p row.

Row 13: (k1, k2tog) five times, k1 (11).

Rows 14–17: st/st, starting with a p row.

Row 18: p2, p2tog, p3, p2tog, p2 (9).

Row 19: join in white yarn and (k1 white, k1 black) to end.

Row 20: break off black yarn and p with white yarn only.

Rows 21–23: st/st, starting with a k row.

Break yarn, draw through sts, pull tightly and fasten off.

Beak

Using yellow yarn, cast on 3 sts.

Row 1: p.

Row 2: k1, k2tog. Slip the first st over the second st and fasten off. Hide the fasten-off end yarn inside the beak and pull gently to curve the beak.

Wings: make two

With black yarn, cast on 10 sts.

Rows 1–5: st/st, starting with a p row.

Row 6: (k1, k2tog) three times, k1 (7).

Rows 7–9: st/st, starting with a p row.

Row 10: (k1, k2tog) twice, k1 (5).

Row 11: p.

Break yarn, draw through sts, pull tightly and fasten off.

Making up

Sew up the body and head following the instructions given for the stork (see page 60). Sew up and attach the wings and also attach the beak. Embroider a French knot for each eye using black DK (8-ply) yarn. To create the feet, sew three small straight stitches for each foot at the base of the body, using yellow DK (8-ply) yarn. To make the fluff on the head, back stitch a few times with white yarn, leaving a loop every other stitch. Cut the loops.

Stork

Instructions

Body and head

Starting with the base, cast on 6 sts with white yarn.

Row 1: kf/b in every st (12).

Row 2: p.

Row 3: (k1, kf/b) to end (18).

Row 4: k for fold line.

Rows 5–6: st/st, starting with a k row.

Row 7: k2tog, k to last 2 sts, k2tog (16).

Rows 8–12: st/st, starting with a p row.

Row 13: (k1, k2tog) five times, k1 (11).

Rows 14–17: st/st, starting with a p row.

Row 18: (p2tog) five times, p1 (6).

Rows 19–26: st/st, starting with a k row.

Row 27: k1, kf/b, k2, kf/b, k1 (8).

Rows 28–30: change to pink yarn and st/st.

Row 31: (k2tog) four times (4).

Break yarn, draw through sts, pull tightly and fasten off.

Beak

Cast on 3 sts with yellow yarn, and work as an i-cord (see page 22).

Rows 1–3: k.

Row 4: k1, k2tog (2).

Rows 5–6: k.

Row 7: k2tog (1).

Row 8: k.

Fasten off.

Wings: make two

The first four rows are knitted double with both black and white fingering (4-ply) yarn knitted together, or two strands taken from black and two strands taken from white DK (8-ply) knitted together, for a marbled effect. Alternatively, work these four rows with black DK (8-ply) yarn only.

Cast on 8 sts with both black and white fingering (4-ply) yarn.

Rows 1–4: st/st, starting with a p row.

Row 5: change to white DK (8-ply) yarn and p.

Row 6: k1, k2tog, k2, k2tog, k1 (6).

Rows 7–8: st/st, starting with a p row.

Row 9: change to pink DK (8-ply) yarn and p.

Row 10: (k1, k2tog) twice (4).

Row 11: p.

Break yarn, draw through sts, pull tightly and fasten off.

Making up

Using the cast-on yarn end, gather through every stitch along the first row, pull tightly and fasten off. Sew the side edges from the bottom to the head, leaving enough space for stuffing. Stuff and close the seam. Work a gathering thread through the back of the neck to shape. Thread a length of yarn through the centre of the base to the back of the neck and back again, twice. Pull gently to flatten the base for stability. Attach the beak then sew up and attach the wings. Embroider a French knot for each eye with black fingering (4-ply) yarn or two strands taken from black DK (8-ply) yarn.

Materials

DK (8-ply) yarn: small amounts of white, pink and yellow

Fingering (4-ply) yarn: small amounts of black and white or two strands taken from each colour of DK (8-ply) yarn

Stuffing

Size

5cm (2in) high, 4cm (1½in) wide

Difficulty level

Intermediate

Owl

Instructions

Body and head

Starting with the base, cast on 5 sts with light brown yarn.

Row 1: kf/b in every st (10).

Row 2: p.

Row 3: (k1, kf/b) to end (15).

Row 4: k for fold line.

Row 5: k.

Row 6: p.

Row 7: k2tog, k to last 2 sts, k2tog (13).

Row 8: p.

Row 9: k1, (k2tog, k1) to end (9).

Rows 10–14: st/st.

Row 15: (k1, k2tog) to end (6).

Break yarn, draw through sts, pull tightly and fasten off.

Beak

With fingering (4-ply) yellow yarn or two strands taken from yellow DK (8-ply) yarn, cast on 3 sts.

Row 1: p.

Row 2: k1, k2tog. Slip the first st over the second st and fasten off.

Hide the fasten-off end yarn inside the beak and pull to curve the beak.

Wings: make two

With a blend of dark and light brown yarn, cast on 6 sts.

Rows 1–3: st/st, starting with a p row.

Row 4: k1, (k2tog) twice, k1 (4).

Row 5: p.

Row 6: (k2tog) twice (2).

Fasten off.

Eyes: make two

Cast on 8 sts with white fingering (4-ply) yarn or two strands taken from white DK (8-ply) yarn. Break yarn, draw through sts, pull tightly and fasten off. Following the instructions given on page 23, make it into a circle.

Making up

Using the cast-on yarn tail, gather through every stitch along the base of the body and head, pull tightly and fasten off. Using the yarn tail at the fasten-off end, join side edges from the top of the head. Stuff and close the seam. Thread a length of yarn through the centre of the body from the top to the base and pull to flatten the base. Sew up and attach the wings and also attach the beak. Attach the whites of the eyes and embroider the centre of each eye with a French knot, using dark brown fingering (4-ply) yarn or two strands taken from dark brown DK (8-ply) yarn. Embroider the feet – sew three small straight stitches for each foot at the base of the body, using yellow DK (8-ply) yarn. Add short fluff on the top of the head with brown fingering (4-ply) yarn – back stitch a few times with brown yarn, leaving a loop every other stitch. Cut the loops.

Materials

DK (8-ply) yarn: small amounts of light brown and dark brown

DK (8-ply) yarn: small amounts of light brown and dark brown blend

Fingering (4-ply) yarn: small amounts of brown, dark brown, white and yellow or two strands taken from each colour of DK (8-ply) yarn

Stuffing

Size

3cm (1¼in) high, 3cm (1¼in) wide

Difficulty level

Intermediate

Blue tit

Instructions

Body and head

Starting with the base, cast on 5 sts with yellow yarn.

Row 1: kf/b in every st (10).

Row 2: p.

Row 3: (k1, kf/b) to end (15).

Row 4: k (fold line).

Row 5: k.

Row 6: p.

Row 7: k2tog, k to last 2 sts, k2tog (13).

Row 8: p.

Row 9: k1, (k2tog, k1) to end (9).

Row 10: p and break off yellow yarn.

Rows 11–12: change to white yarn and st/st.

Rows 13–14: break off white yarn, change to blue yarn and st/st.

Row 15: (k1, k2tog) to end with blue yarn (6).

Break yarn, draw through sts, pull tightly and fasten off.

Tail

Cast on 3 sts with blue yarn.

Rows 1–3: k.

Row 4: k2tog, k1 (2).

Fasten off.

Wings: make two

Cast on 6 sts with yellow yarn.

Rows 1–3: st/st, starting with a p row.

Row 4: change to blue yarn, (k1, k2tog) to end (4).

Row 5: p.

Break yarn, draw through sts, pull tightly and fasten off.

Making up

Using the cast-on yarn tail, gather through every stitch along the base of the body and head, pull tightly and fasten off. Using the yarn tail at the fasten-off end, join the side edges from the top of the head. Stuff and close the seam. Thread a length of yarn through the centre of the body from the top to the base and pull to flatten the base. Work a gathering thread around the neck and pull tightly to shape the head.

Sew up and attach the wings and also attach the tail. With dark brown DK (8-ply) yarn, create a beak by back stitching on the same spot three times. With dark brown fingering (4-ply) yarn or two strands taken from dark brown DK (8-ply) yarn, work a French knot for each eye and embroider the feet. Sew three small straight stitches for each foot at the base of the body.

Materials

DK (8-ply) yarn: small amounts of yellow, blue, white and dark brown

Fingering (4-ply) yarn: small amount of dark brown, or two strands taken from dark brown DK (8-ply) yarn

Stuffing

Sizes

3cm (1¼in) high, 3cm (1¼in) wide

Difficulty level

Intermediate

Variation

To create a blackbird, use the same pattern but use black yarn for the body, head, wings and tail and embroider the beak and feet with yellow yarn. Work a French knot for each eye with white fingering (4-ply) yarn, or two strands taken from white DK (8-ply) yarn.

Robin and chicks

Instructions

Body and head

Cast on 5 sts with brown yarn.

Row 1: kf/b in every st (10).

Row 2: p.

Row 3: (k1, kf/b) to end (15).

Row 4: k for fold line.

Row 5: k.

Row 6: join in red yarn and p6 (brown), p3 (red), p6 (brown).

Row 7: k2tog, k3 (brown), k5 (red), k3, k2tog (brown) (13).

Row 8: keeping the colours correct, p.

Row 9: k1, k2tog, k1 (brown), k2tog, k1, k2tog (red), k1, k2tog, k1 (brown) (9).

Rows 10–13: keeping the colours correct, st/st.

Row 14: break off red yarn and p with brown yarn only.

Row 15: (k2tog, k1) to end (6). Break off yarn, draw through sts, pull tightly and fasten off.

Beak

Cast on 2 sts with dark brown yarn, purl 1 row, turn. Slip the first st over the second st and fasten off.

Wings: make two

Cast on 6 sts with brown yarn.

Rows 1–3: st/st, starting with a p row.

Row 4: k1, (k2tog) twice, k1 (4).

Row 5: p.

Break yarn, draw through sts, pull tightly and fasten off.

Nest

The nest is tiny, but simple to make. The chicks do not have bodies, just heads.

With a crochet hook and light brown yarn, make a starting ring.

Rnd 1: make 1ch, 6dc (*US sc*) in ring, ss in first dc (*US sc*) to close the ring (6).

Rnd 2: 1ch, 1dc (*US sc*) in the base of the first ch, 2dc (*US sc*) in each dc (*US sc*), ss in first dc (*US sc*) (12).

Rnd 3: 1ch, 1dc (*US sc*) in each dc (*US sc*), ss in first dc (*US sc*) and fasten off.

Chicks: make three

Cast on 10 sts with yellow yarn. Break off yarn, draw through sts, pull tightly and fasten off. Insert the threaded needle back into the sts, taking it out at the cast-on edge. Work a gathering thread along the cast-on edge and pull tightly to make a 'bobble'.

Making up

To make up the robin, follow the instructions given for the blue tit on page 64, omitting the gathering thread around the neck.

To make up the nest, sew up the side seam.

To make up the chicks in the nest, attach their heads to the centre of the nest. With orange fingering (4-ply) yarn, or two strands taken from orange DK (8-ply) yarn, back stitch on the same spot two or three times on each head to create a beak. Work a French knot for each eye with dark brown fingering (4-ply) yarn or two strands taken from dark brown DK (8-ply) yarn.

Woodpecker

Instructions

Sitting woodpecker

Body and head

With black yarn, cast on 5 sts.
Row 1: kf/b in every st (10).
Row 2: p.
Row 3: (k1, kf/b) to end (15).
Row 4: k (fold line).
Row 5: k.
Row 6: p.
Row 7: k2tog, k to last 2 sts, k2tog (13).
Row 8: p.
Row 9: k1, (k2tog, k1) to end (9).
Row 10: p.
Rows 11–12: change to white yarn and st/st.
Rows 13–14: change to black yarn and st/st.
Row 15: change to red yarn and (k1, k2tog) to end (6).
Break yarn, leaving a long end. Draw through sts, pull tightly and fasten off.

Beak

Make 4 chains with a crochet hook and yellow yarn. Fasten off and hide the yarn end inside the beak.

Tail

Cast on 3 sts with black yarn.
Rows 1–3: k.
Row 4: k2tog, k1 (2).
Pass the first st over the second st and fasten off.

Wings: make two

Cast on 6 sts with black yarn.
Rows 1–3: st/st, starting with a p row.
Row 4: (k1, k2tog) to end (4).
Row 5: p.
Break yarn, draw through sts, pull tightly and fasten off.

Making up

Using the cast-on yarn tail, gather through every stitch along the base of the body and head, pull tightly and fasten off. Using the yarn tail at the fasten-off end, join the side edges from the top of the head. Stuff and close the seam. Thread a length of yarn through the centre of the body from the top of the head to the base and pull to flatten. Work a gathering thread around the neck and pull tightly to shape the head.
Attach the tail and beak. Sew up the wings and attach them. To make the fluff on the head, back stitch a few times with red yarn, leaving a loop every other stitch. Cut the loops. Work a French knot for each eye with dark brown fingering (4-ply) yarn or two strands taken from dark brown DK (8-ply) yarn. To create the feet, sew three small straight stitches for each foot at the base of the body, using yellow DK (8-ply) yarn.

Materials

DK (8-ply) yarn: small amounts of red, black, white and yellow

Fingering (4-ply) yarn: small amount of dark brown or two strands taken from dark brown DK (8-ply) yarn

Stuffing

Additional equipment

3mm (US C/2 or D/3, UK 11) crochet hook

Size

4cm (1½in) high, 2.5cm (1in) wide

Difficulty level

Intermediate

Woodpecker in tree

Body and head

Cast on 9 sts with black yarn.

Rows 1–7: st/st, starting with a p row.

Rows 8–9: change to white yarn and st/st.

Rows 10–11: change to black yarn and st/st.

Row 12: change to red yarn and (k1, k2tog) to end (6).

Break off yarn, leaving a long end. Draw through sts, pull tightly and fasten off.

Wings, beak and tail

Follow instructions given for the sitting woodpecker.

Making up

Sew the body and head from both the tail and the head ends, stuff the body and head and close the seam. Attach the tail and beak. Sew up the wings and attach them. Make the fluff on the head as for the sitting woodpecker. Work a French knot for each eye with dark brown fingering (4-ply) yarn or two strands taken from dark brown DK (8-ply) yarn. To create the feet, sew three small straight stitches for each foot at the base of the body, using yellow DK (8-ply) yarn.

Hare

Instructions

Body and legs

Cast on 13 sts with white or brown yarn, st/st 15 rows.
Cast off.

Head

Cast on 11 sts with white or brown yarn.
Rows 1–4: st/st, starting with a p row.
Row 5: p2, (p1, p2tog) to end (8).
Break yarn, draw through sts, pull tightly and fasten off.

Ears: make two

Cast on 3 sts with white or brown yarn.
Rows 1–4: st/st, starting with a p row.
Row 5: p1, p2tog (2).
Row 6: k2tog (1).
Fasten off.

Making up

Fold the corners of the body towards each other. Sew them from the tips towards the centre to create four legs. Stuff and close the tummy. Using the yarn from the fasten-off end, sew the head. Stuff and close the seam. Attach the head to the body. Attach ears. Embroider a French knot for each eye and small straight stitches for the nose using dark brown fingering (4-ply) yarn or two strands taken from dark brown DK (8-ply) yarn. With white or brown yarn, back stitch on the same spot a few times to create a bobble for the tail. For a visual guide, see the instructions on page 19.

Materials

DK (8-ply) yarn: small amount of white or brown

Fingering (4-ply) yarn: small amount of dark brown or two strands taken from dark brown DK (8-ply) yarn

Stuffing

Size

5cm (2in) high,
4cm (1½in) wide

Difficulty level

Intermediate

Hedgehog

Instructions

Head

Cast on 7 sts with light
brown yarn.
Rows 1–3: st/st, starting with
a p row.
Row 4: (k1, k2tog) twice, k1 (5).
Row 5: p2tog, p1, p2tog (3).
Row 6: k.
Break yarn, draw through sts, pull
tightly and fasten off.

Making up

Cut a piece of card 2 x 3cm (¾
x 1¼in). Wind dark grey fingering
(4-ply) yarn around it about
twenty-five times and make a
pompom. Attach the head to
the pompom and embroider a
French knot for each eye with dark
brown fingering (4-ply) yarn or two
strands taken from dark brown DK
(8-ply) yarn. Using the same yarn,
create a nose by back stitching a
few times in the same place.

Materials

DK (8-ply) yarn: small amount
of light brown

Fingering (4-ply) yarn: small
amount of dark grey

Fingering (4-ply) yarn: small
amount of dark brown or
two strands taken from
dark brown DK (8-ply) yarn

Strong cotton thread for
making pompom

Size

3cm (1¼in) wide,
2cm (¾in) high

Difficulty level

Beginner

Mouse

Instructions

Body and head

Starting with the base, cast on 4 sts with white yarn.
Row 1: kf/b in every st (8).
Rows 2–5: st/st, starting with a p row.
Row 6: (p1, p2tog) to last 2 sts, p2 (6).
Break yarn, draw through sts, pull tightly and
fasten off.

Making up

Sew the body and stuff. Thread a length of yarn
through the centre of the body from the top to the
bottom and pull to flatten the base. Create ears by
back stitching on the same spot three times with
white DK (8-ply) yarn. Take out the yarn end to
make a tail, tying the end with a knot. Embroider
tiny straight stitches to create the eyes and nose
with dark brown fingering (4-ply) yarn or two strands
taken from dark brown DK (8-ply) yarn.

Materials

DK (8-ply) yarn: small
amount of white

Fingering (4-ply) yarn: small
amount of dark brown or
two strands taken from
dark brown DK (8-ply)
yarn

Size

1cm (½in) high, 1cm (½in)
long, plus length of tail

Difficulty level

Beginner

Squirrel

Instructions

Body and legs

Cast on 11 sts with light grey yarn and st/st 12 rows.
Cast off.

Head

Cast on 8 sts with light grey yarn and st/st 3 rows, starting with a p row.
Next row: k1, k2tog, k2, k2tog, k1 (6).
Break yarn, draw through sts, pull tightly and fasten off.

Ears: make two

Cast on 2 sts with 2 strands taken from light grey DK (8-ply) yarn and knit 1 row.
Slip the first st over the second st and fasten off.

Tail

Wind light grey DK (8-ply) yarn around two fingers about 25 times and make a pompom. Try to cut it so that it forms a slightly oblong shape.

Making up

Follow the instructions given for the hare (page 70). Attach the head, ears, and the tail. Embroider a French knot for each eye with dark brown fingering (4-ply) yarn or two strands taken from dark brown DK (8-ply) yarn. If you want to embroider a nose, back stitch on the same spot a few times using dark brown fingering (4-ply) yarn or two strands taken from dark brown DK (8-ply) yarn.

Acorn

Cast on 4 sts with light brown DK (8-ply) yarn and purl 1 row. Break yarn, draw through sts, pull tightly and fasten off.

Variation

Use red-brown yarn to create a red squirrel.

Materials

DK (8-ply) yarn: small amount of light grey and light brown

Fingering (4-ply) yarn: small amount of dark brown or two strands taken from dark brown DK (8-ply) yarn

Stuffing

Strong cotton thread for making pompom

Size

3cm (1¼in) high,
4cm (1½in) wide

Difficulty level

Intermediate

Mole

Instructions

Mole

Body and head

Starting at the tail end, cast on 6 sts with dark grey yarn.
Row 1: kf/b in every st (12).
Rows 2–4: st/st, starting with a p row.
Row 5: (k1, k2tog) to end (8).
Row 6: p.
Row 7: k1, k2tog, k2, k2tog, k1 (6).
Row 8: (p2tog) to end (3).
Row 9: k.
Break yarn, draw through sts, pull tightly and fasten off.

Tail

Using dark grey DK (8-ply) yarn make 3 chains with a crochet hook and fasten off. Hide the fasten-off yarn end inside the tail

Making up

Sew the body and head, stuff and close the seam. Attach the tail. Embroider the nose with pink yarn by back stitching a few times on the same spot. With beige yarn, create feet by back stitching on the same spot three times. Embroider a tiny stitch for each eye with dark brown fingering (4-ply) yarn or two strands taken from DK (8-ply) yarn.

Mole in the ground

Head

Follow the instructions given for the hedgehog (see page 72) but with dark grey yarn.

Soil

With a crochet hook and brown yarn, *make 3 chains, 3dc (US sc) in the first ch, repeat from* five more times.
Fasten off.

Making up

Sew the head, stuff and close the seam. Embroider the nose with back stitch using pink yarn. Wrap the crochet soil around the mole and secure it with a few stitches. Embroider the paws with back stitch using beige yarn. Embroider a tiny stitch for each eye with dark brown fingering (4-ply) yarn or two strands taken from DK (8-ply) yarn.

Materials

Mole:

DK (8-ply) yarn: small amounts of dark grey, dark brown, pink, and beige

Fingering (4-ply) yarn: small amount of dark brown or two strands taken from dark brown DK (8-ply) yarn

Stuffing

Mole in the ground:

DK (8-ply) yarn: small amounts of dark grey, beige, pink and brown

Fingering (4-ply) yarn: small amount of dark brown or two strands taken from dark brown DK (8-ply) yarn

Stuffing

Additional equipment

3mm (US C/2 or D/3, UK 11) crochet hook

Size

Mole: 3.5cm (1⅜in) high, 1.5cm (½in) wide

Mole in the ground: 2cm (¾in) high, 2cm (¾in) wide

Difficulty level

Beginner

Turtle

Instructions

Knitted turtle

The top and bottom shells are knitted as one piece.

Shell

Starting with the base, cast on 5 sts with green yarn.
Row 1: kf/b in every st (10).
Row 2: p.
Row 3: (k1, kf/b) to end (15).
Row 4: k for fold line.
Rows 5–9: st/st, starting with a k row.
Row 10: (p3, p2tog) to end (12).
Row 11: (k2tog) to end (6).
Break yarn, draw through sts, pull tightly and fasten off.

Head and neck

Cast on 4 sts with brown yarn.
Work as an i-cord (see page 22) for 4 rows.
Row 5: k1, kf/b two times, k1 (6).
Break yarn, draw through sts, pull tightly and fasten off.

Making up

Using the yarn tail at the fasten-off end, sew the top shell seam. Using the cast-on yarn tail, gather through every st along the first row and pull tightly. Stuff and close the seam. Thread a length of yarn through the centre of the bottom shell to the centre of the top shell. Repeat once more and pull gently to flatten the base. Embroider the legs and tail using brown DK (8-ply) yarn and by back stitching on the same spot three times. Embroider a French knot for each eye with dark brown fingering (4-ply) yarn, or two strands taken from dark brown DK (8-ply) yarn.

Crocheted turtle

The shell is crocheted; the head and neck are worked as an i-cord.

Top shell

Make a starting ring with green yarn.
Rnd 1: ch1, 7dc (*US sc*) into the ring, ss to first dc (*US sc*).
Rnd 2: make 1ch, 2dc (*US sc*) in each dc (*US sc*), ss in first dc (*US sc*) (14).
Rnd 3: make 1ch, 1dc (*US sc*) in each dc (*US sc*), ss in first dc (*US sc*).
Rnd 4: ss in each dc (*US sc*).
Fasten off.

Bottom shell

Follow the instructions given for the top shell to rnd 2. Fasten off.

Head and neck

Follow the instructions given for the knitted turtle.

Making up

Sew the top and bottom shells together, leaving a small opening for stuffing. Stuff all the yarn ends inside the shells, and a bit of wool stuffing if you need to create a round, full shape. Attach the head. Embroider the legs and tail using brown DK (8-ply) yarn and by back stitching on the same spot three times. Embroider a French knot for each eye with dark brown fingering (4-ply) yarn, or two strands taken from dark brown DK (8-ply) yarn.

Materials

Each turtle:

DK (8-ply) yarn: small amounts of green and brown

Fingering (4-ply) yarn: small amount of dark brown yarn or two strands taken from dark brown DK (8-ply) yarn

Stuffing

Additional equipment

3mm (US C/2 or D/3, UK 11) crochet hook

Size

3cm (1¼in) long, 2cm (¾in) high

Difficulty level

Beginner

Gnome

Instructions

Body and head

Starting with the base, cast on 6 sts with blue yarn.

Row 1: p.

Row 2: kf/b in every st (12).

Row 3: p.

Row 4: (k1, kf/b) to end (18).

Row 5: k for fold line.

Rows 6–7: st/st, starting with a k row.

Row 8: k2, (k2tog, k2) to end (14).

Rows 9–13: st/st.

Row 14: (k1, k2tog) to last 2 sts, k2 (10).

Break off yarn.

Row 15: join in beige yarn and p.

Row 16: (k1, kf/b) to end (15).

Rows 17–21: st/st.

Row 22: (k1, k2tog) to end (10).

Break yarn, draw through sts, pull tightly and fasten off. Leave a long tail for sewing up later.

Arms: make two

Cast on 4 sts with blue yarn and work as an i-cord for four rows (see page 22).

Change to beige yarn and work two more rows as an i-cord. Break yarn, draw through sts and fasten off. Hide yarn ends inside the arm.

Belt

Work 20 chains with a crochet hook using grey DK (8-ply) yarn.

Hat

Cast on 14 sts with red yarn.

Rows 1–9: st/st, starting with a k row.

Row 10: p2tog, (p1, p2tog) to end (9).

Rows 11–12: st/st.

Break yarn, draw through sts, pull tightly and fasten off.

Boots: make two

Cast on 9 sts with dark brown yarn.

Rows 1–3: p.

Row 4: k.

Row 5: p.

Row 6: k3, cast off next 3 sts, k to end (6).

Row 7: (p1, pf/b) four times, p1 (10).

Row 8: cast off.

Beard

Using fine grey bouclé yarn, cast on 8 sts.

Row 1: k.

Row 2: skpo, k to last 2 sts, k2tog (6).

Row 3: k.

Row 4: skpo, k to last 2 sts, k2tog (4).

Row 5: k.

Row 6: skpo, k2tog (2).

Fasten off.

Materials

DK (8-ply) yarn: small amounts of blue, red, beige, grey and dark brown

Fine bouclé yarn: small amounts of fine grey or two strands taken from grey DK (8-ply) yarn

Fingering (4-ply) yarn: small amount of dark brown or two strands taken from dark brown DK (8-ply) yarn

Stuffing

Additional equipment

3mm (US C/2 or D/3, UK 11) crochet hook

Size

7cm (2¾in) high, 3.5cm (1³⁄₈in) wide

Difficulty level

Intermediate

Making up

Body and head: using the cast-on yarn tail, thread through every st and pull tightly to gather the base of the body. Sew the rest of the base. Using the yarn at the fasten-off end, sew the head seam as far as the neck. Leave the yarn uncut. Sew the body seam from the neck down with blue yarn, leaving enough space for stuffing. Stuff the body and head and close the seam. Using the beige yarn left from the head, work a gathering thread through every stitch along the base of the head and pull tightly to create a neck.

Boots: Work a gathering thread through every stitch along the base of each boot, pull tightly. Sew the rest of the base and then join side edges. Close the hole at the top of the foot and stuff. Leave the top end open. Attach the boots to the base of the body.

Sew the hat seam using the fasten-off end and attach to the head. Also attach the arms, beard and belt. Create a belt buckle using two straight back stitches in brown DK (8-ply) yarn.

Create the nose by back stitching on the same spot three times with beige DK (8-ply) yarn. Work a French knot for each eye using dark brown fingering (4-ply) yarn, or two strands taken from dark brown DK (8-ply) yarn.

Toadstool house

Instructions

Cap

Starting with the base, cast on 13 sts with white yarn.
Row 1: p.
Row 2: kf/b in every st (26).
Row 3: p.
Row 4: (kf/b, k1) to end (39).
Row 5: p.
Row 6: (k1, kf/b, k1) to end (52).
Row 7: p.
Row 8: change to red yarn and k.
Row 9: k for edge.
Divide stitches onto three double-pointed needles and work in rounds.
Rnds 1–10: k.
Rnd 11: (k1, k2tog) to last st, k1 (35).
Rnds 12–19: k.
Rnd 20: (k2tog) to last st, k1 (18).
Rnds 21–22: k.
Break yarn, draw through sts, pull tightly and fasten off.

Stalk

With white yarn, cast on 6 sts.
Row 1: kf/b in every st (12).
Row 2: p.
Row 3: (k1, kf/b) to end (18).
Row 4: p.
Row 5: (k2, kf/b) to end (24).
Row 6: p.
Row 7: (k1, kf/b, k1) to end (32).
Row 8: k for fold line.
Rows 9–18: st/st, starting with a k row.
Row 19: (k1, k2tog, k1) to end (24).
Rows 20–24: st/st.
Cast off.

Door

With brown yarn, cast on 7 sts
Rows 1–3: st/st, starting with a p row.
Row 4: k, dec 1 st on both ends (5).
Rows 5–6: st/st.
Cast off.

Chimney

With brown yarn, cast on 10 sts and st/st 7 rows.
K1 row.
Cast off.

Materials

DK (8-ply) yarn: 10g (¹⁄₃oz), red, 10g (¹⁄₃oz), white

DK (8-ply) yarn: small amounts of brown, dark brown and colours of your choice for the flowers

Stuffing

Size

9cm (3½in) tall, 4cm (1½in) diameter of stalk

Difficulty level

Beginner

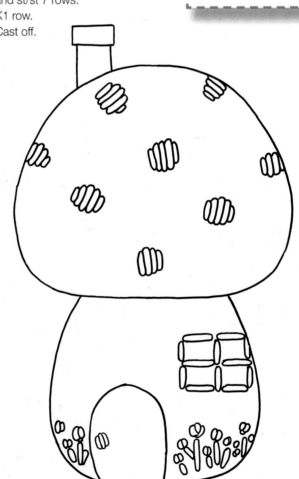

Making up

Sew the seam of the cap, stuff and close the seam. Sew the stalk from the cast-on end and stuff, keeping the cast-off end open. Attach the cap to the stalk sewing them together all around.

Sew the side seam of the chimney from the cast-on end to the cast off end. Attach the chimney to the roof by its cast-on end, leaving the cast-off end open. Lightly stuff the chimney, then close up the top with a few stitches. Attach the door. Embroider the window, door handle, dots on the cap and flowers using DK (8-ply) yarn in your choice of colours and stitches – see embroidery drawing, left.

Make a small mushroom, following the pattern on page 85. Attach it to the side of the house.

Tip

If you do not want to knit in rounds after row 9, keep working in st/st with two needles and sew the edges together at the end.

Mushrooms

Materials

DK (8-ply) yarn: small amounts of red and white

Stuffing

Size

Large: 4cm (1½in) diameter, 4cm (1½in) high

Medium: 3cm (1¼in) diameter, 3cm (1¼in) high

Small: 2cm (¾in) diameter, 3cm (1¼in) high

Difficulty level

Beginner

Instructions

Large

Cap

Cast on 6 sts with white yarn.
Row 1: p.
Row 2: kf/b in every st (12).
Row 3: p.
Row 4: (k1, kf/b) to end (18).
Row 5: p.
Row 6: (k1, kf/b) to end (27).
Row 7: p.
Row 8: change to red yarn and k.
Row 9: k for the edge.
Rows 10–16: st/st, starting with a k row.
Row 17: (p1, p2tog) to end (18).
Row 18: k.
Row 19: (p1, p2tog) to end (12).
Break yarn, draw through sts, pull tightly and fasten off.

Stalk

Cast on 6 sts with white yarn.
Row 1: kf/b in every st (12).
Row 2: k for the edge.
Rows 3–10: st/st, starting with a k row.
Row 11: (k2tog, k1) to end (8).
Cast off.

Medium

Cap

Cast on 7 sts with white yarn.
Row 1: p.
Row 2: kf/b in every st (14).
Row 3: p.
Row 4: (k1, kf/b) to end (21).
Row 5: p.
Row 6: change to red yarn and k.
Row 7: k for the edge.
Rows 8–13: st/st, starting with a k row.
Row 14: (k1, k2tog) to end (14).
Row 15: p.
Row 16: (k2tog) to end (7).
Break yarn, draw through sts, pull tightly and fasten off.

Stalk

Cast on 6 sts with white yarn.
Row 1: kf/b in every st (12).
Row 2: k for the edge.
Rows 3–7: st/st, starting with a k row.
Row 8: (p2tog, p1) to end (8).
Cast off.

Small

Cap

Cast on 7 sts with white yarn.
Row 1: kf/b in every st (14).
Rows 2–3: st/st.
Row 4: change to red yarn and p.
Row 5: p for the edge.
Rows 6–10: st/st, starting with a p row.
Row 11: (k2tog) to end (7).
Break yarn, draw through sts, pull tightly and fasten off.

Stalk

With white yarn, cast on 4 sts.
Row 1: kf/b in every st (8).
Row 2: k for the edge.
Rows 3–6: st/st, starting with a k row.
Row 7: k2tog, (k1, k2tog) to end (5).
Cast off.

Making up

Make up each mushroom in the same way. Sew the side seam of the cap from the fasten-off end, stopping at where the colour changes. Using the yarn tail at the cast-on end, work a gathering thread through each st and pull tightly. Stuff the cap and close the seam. Thread a length of yarn through the centre of the cap from the base to the top and pull the yarn to flatten the base. For the stalk, work a gathering thread through each st of the base, pull tightly and sew the rest of the seam. Stuff the stalk and flatten the base in the same way as for the base of the cap. Sew it in position. Create dots on the mushroom caps by sewing several back stitches on top of each other, using white DK (8-ply) yarn.

Tip:
You can change the height by changing the number of rows you work for the stalk.

Tree

Instructions

The tree trunk is knitted flat from the top. If you are skilled with circular needles, you can use them and knit in rounds from row 1 to row 63.

Trunk

Cast on 6 sts with brown yarn.
Row 1: p.
Row 2: (k1, kf/b) to end (9).
Rows 3–5: st/st.
Row 6: (k1, kf/b) to last st, k1 (13).
Rows 7-9: st/st.
Row 10: (k2, kf/b) to last st, k1 (17).
Rows 11–20: st/st.
Row 21: k2, (kf/b, k2) to end (22).
Rows 22–31: st/st.
Row 32: (k2, kf/b) to last st, k1 (29).
Rows 33–43: st/st.
Row 44: k2, (kf/b, k2) to end (38).
Rows 45–53: st/st.
Row 54: (k8, kf/b) four times, k2 (42).
Rows 55–63: st/st.
You are working on the roots of the tree from this point on.
Row 1: k7, turn. Work on this set of sts only.
Rows 2–4: st/st, starting with a p row.
Row 5: skpo, k3, k2tog (5).
Row 6: p.
Row 7: skpo, k1, k2tog (3).
Row 8: p.
Row 9: skpo, k1 (2).
Row 10: p2tog (1).
Row 11: kf/b (2).

Row 12: p.
Row 13: k1, kf/b (3).
Row 14: p.
Row 15: kf/b, k1, kf/b (5).
Row 16: p.
Row 17: kf/b, k3, kf/b (7).
Rows 18–20: st/st.
Row 21: k the 7 sts you have been working on. Do not break the yarn, then knit the next 7 sts from the main section. Working on this set of 7 sts only, repeat rows 2–21.
Repeat rows 2–21 four more times to make six roots in total.
When you have knitted all the root pieces, continue as follows:
Row 22: p across all 42 stitches (42).
Do not worry if the sets of 7 sts are not well connected or if the connecting yarn is a little loose.
Row 23: (k4, k2tog) to end (35).
Row 24: p.
Row 25: (k3, k2tog) to end (28).
Row 26: p.
Row 27: (k2, k2tog) to end (21).
Row 28: p.
Row 29: (k1, k2tog) to end (14).
Row 30: p.
Row 31: (k2tog) to end (7).
Break yarn, draw through sts, pull tightly and fasten off.

Materials

To make one tree:

DK (8-ply) yarn: 25g (1oz), brown

Fingering (4-ply) yarn: 20g (¾oz) green or two strands taken from green DK (8-ply) yarn

Stuffing

Ceramic baking beans

Cardboard

Size

15cm (6in) tall, 10cm (4in) base diameter, 15cm (6in) diameter at widest point

Difficulty level

Intermediate

Branch, large

Cast on 6 sts with brown yarn.
Rows 1–6: st/st, starting with
a k row.
Row 7: (k1, kf/b) three times (9).
Rows 8–14: st/st.
Row 15: (k2, kf/b) to end (12).
Rows 16–24: st/st.
Row 25: (k2, kf/b) to end (16).
Rows 26–34: st/st.
Cast off.

Branch, small

Cast on 6 sts with brown yarn.
Rows 1–6: st/st, starting with
a k row.
Row 7: (k1, kf/b) three times (9).
Rows 8–14: st/st.
Row 15: (k2, kf/b) to end (12).
Rows 16–24: st/st.
Cast off.

Making up

Sew up the trunk seam. Starting
at the top, fill the top half of the
tree with stuffing and the bottom
half with ceramic baking beans.
Use the star-shaped template,
see right, to create a cardboard
shape. Insert the cardboard shape
and sew up the base. Sew the
seam of each branch and stuff.
Sew the branches to the trunk.
With fine green fingering (4-ply)
yarn, back stitch all over the ends
of the branches, leaving a loop
every other stitch. Cut the loops to
create the fluffy foliage.

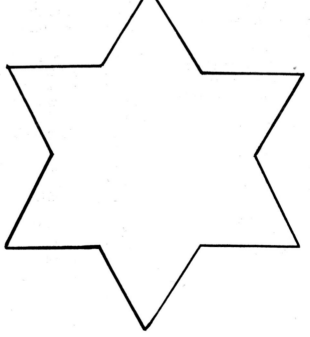

87

Tree stump

Instructions

Crocheted tree stump

The top piece is crocheted and the roots are knitted with stitches picked up from the crochet edge. With a crochet hook, work as follows:

Top piece

Wind light brown yarn around your finger to form a starting ring.

Rnd 1: 1ch, 8dc (*US sc*) into ring, ss in first dc (*US sc*) (8).

Rnd 2: 1ch, 2dc (*US sc*) in each dc (*US sc*), ss in first dc (*US sc*) (16).

Rnd 3: 1ch, 1dc (*US sc*) in same place as ss, (2dc/*US sc* in next dc/*US sc*, 1dc/*US sc* in next dc/*US sc*) seven times, 2dc (*US sc*) in last dc (*US sc*), ss in first dc (*US sc*) (24).

Rnd 4: 1ch, 1dc (*US sc*) in same place as ss, 1dc (*US sc*) in next dc (*US sc*) (2dc/*US sc* in next dc/*US sc*, 1dc/*US sc* in each of next 2dc/*US sc*) seven times, 2dc (*US sc*) in last dc (*US sc*), ss in first dc (*US sc*) (32).

Rnd 5: 1ch, 1dc (*US sc*) in same place as ss, 1dc (*US sc*) in each of next 2dc (*US sc*), (2dc/*US sc* in next dc/*US sc*, 1dc/*US sc* in each of next 3dc/*US sc*) seven times, 2dc (*US sc*) in last dc (*US sc*), ss in first dc (*US sc*) (40).

Rnd 6: 1ch, 1dc (*US sc*) in same place as ss, (1dc/*US sc* in each of next 12dc/*US sc*, 2dc/*US sc* in next dc/*US sc*) three times (43).

Rnd 7: 1dc (*US sc*) in each dc (*US sc*). Fasten off.

With brown DK (8-ply) yarn, pick up 42 sts from the outer edge of the top piece and divide them onto 3 short 2.75mm (UK 12, US 2) double-pointed knitting needles. Knit 8 rounds.

Roots

You are working on the roots from this point on.

Change to a pair of 2.75mm (UK 12, US 2) knitting needles and work flat as follows:

Row 1: k7, turn. Work on this set of 7 sts only.

Rows 2–4: st/st, starting with a p row.

Row 5: skpo, k3, k2tog (5).

Row 6: p.

Row 7: skpo, k1, k2tog (3).

Row 8: p.

Row 9: skpo, k1 (2).

Row 10: p2tog (1).

Row 11: kf/b (2).

Row 12: p.

Row 13: k1, kf/b (3).

Row 14: p.

Row 15: kf/b, k1, kf/b (5).

Row 16: p.

Row 17: kf/b, k3, kf/b (7).

Rows 18–20: st/st.

Row 21: k the 7 sts you have been working on. Do not break the yarn, then knit the next 7 sts from the main section. Working on this set of 7 sts only, repeat rows 2–21.

Repeat rows 2–21 four more times to make 6 roots in total.

When you have knitted all the root pieces, continue as follows:

Row 22: p across all 42 stitches (42).

Do not worry if the sets of 7 sts

Materials

DK (8-ply) yarn: 10g ($^{1}/_{3}$oz), brown

DK (8-ply) yarn: 4g ($^{1}/_{8}$oz), light brown

Stuffing

Additional equipment

2.75mm (UK 12, US 2) knitting or circular needles x 4

3mm (US C/2 or D/3, UK 11) crochet hook

Size

6cm (2½in) diameter of top

Difficulty level

Intermediate

are not well connected or if the connecting yarn is a little loose.

Row 23: (k4, k2tog) to end (35).

Row 24: p.

Row 25: (k3, k2tog) to end (28).

Row 26: p.

Row 27: (k2, k2tog) to end (21).

Row 28: p.

Row 29: (k1, k2tog) to end (14).

Row 30: p.

Row 31: (k2tog) to end (7).

Break yarn, draw through sts, pull tightly and fasten off.

Making up

Sew the piece together, leaving a small opening for stuffing. Stuff and close the seam. Thread a length of light brown yarn through the centre of the stump to the centre of the top and back again twice, to flatten the top.

Knitted tree stump

Starting with the top piece, cast on 7 sts with light brown yarn.

Row 1: kf/b in every st (14).
Row 2: p.
Row 3: (k1, kf/b) to end (21).
Row 4: p.
Row 5: (k2, kf/b) to end (28).
Row 6: p.
Row 7: (k3, kf/b) to end (35).
Row 8: p.
Row 9: (k4, kf/b) to end (42).
Row 10: k for edge.
Rows 11–18: change to brown yarn and st/st, starting with a k row.
Follow rows 1–31 given for the crocheted tree stump.

Making up

Follow the intructions given for the crocheted tree stump.

Forest floor

Instructions

The mat is a patchwork of many knitted squares. It is a very relaxed project. You can make squares of any size with any yarn. You can experiment with some new stitch patterns. This project also provides a good opportunity to practise knitting for beginners. If you use stocking stitch, from beginning to end, the edges will curl. To stop this from happening, use garter or moss stitches on the four edges. Knit and keep making squares. You can change colours or stitch patterns without breaking the yarn. When you think you have made about 70 per cent of the mat, press each square with an iron, then arrange and sew the squares together. See how many more squares you need and in what size and make more squares to fill in the space. Here are some suggestions for squares:

Square A

Cast on 22 sts, knit every row until the work measures 6cm (2½in). Cast off.

Square B

Cast on 22 sts, and knit 1 row.
Next row: k3, (k1, p1) to last 3 sts, k3.
Repeat this row until the work measures 6cm (2½in). Knit 1 row. Cast off.

Square C

Cast on 25 sts, and knit 2 rows.
Row 1: (k5, p5) twice, k5.
Row 2: (p5, k5) twice, p5.
Rows 3 and 5: same as row 1.
Rows 4 and 6: same as row 2.
Row 7: (p5, k5) twice, p5.
Row 8: (k5, p5) twice, k5.
Rows 9 and 11: same as row 7.
Rows 10 and 12: same as row 8.
Repeat rows 1–12 twice more.
Knit 2 rows.
Cast off.

Square D

Cast on 21 sts.
Row 1: k.
Row 2: k2, p17, k2.
Repeat last 2 rows until the work measures 5cm (2in). Knit 1 row.

Grass

Thread a needle with green yarn. Use fingering (4-ply) yarn if you have it, but two strands taken from DK (8-ply) yarn will also work well. Bring the needle through from the back to the front of the mat. Use a back stitch to secure the yarn end. Back stitch on the same spot again, leaving a long loop, then again without leaving a loop. Repeat this process until you are happy with the quantity of green loops. Cut all the loops.

Materials

Any yarn of your choice. The quantity of yarn depends on how big you would like the mat to be. To make a 40 x 40cm (16 x16in) mat you will need about 200g (7oz) of DK (8-ply) yarn in total

Fingering (4-ply) yarn: small amount of green, or a few strands taken from green DK (8-ply)

Any yarn: small amounts of red, yellow and pink or colours of your choice for flowers

Difficulty level

Beginner

Flowers

Make a knot with any yarn and colour of your choice. Hide the yarn ends inside the knot. Thread a needle with green fingering (4-ply) yarn, or two strands taken from green DK (8-ply) yarn and bring it through the knot. Attach the knot to the mat where you have sewn the grass. Alternatively, make a French knot directly onto the mat.

See overleaf for instructions for creating ponds and rocks.

Materials

To make 3 i-cord ponds or 3 crochet ponds:

DK (8-ply) yarn: 25g (1oz), blue yarn

Additional equipment

A pair of 3mm (US 2 or 3, UK 11) knitting needles

Darning needle

3mm (US C/2 or D/3, UK 11) crochet hook

Size

6–7cm (2½–2¾in) diameter

Difficulty level

Beginner

I-cord pond

Cast on 2sts with blue yarn and work an i-cord (see page 22) for 80cm–1m (32–39in). Roll it up from the end and secure with a few stitches.

Crochet pond

Make a starting ring with blue yarn.

Rnd 1: 1ch, 6dc (*US sc*) in ring, ss in first dc (*US sc*) and close the ring (6).

Rnd 2: 1ch, 2dc (*US sc*) in each dc (*US sc*), ss in first dc (*US sc*) (12).

Rnd 3: 1ch, 1dc (*US sc*) in same place as ss, (2dc/*US sc* in next dc/*US sc*, 1dc/*US sc* in next dc/*US sc*) five times, 2dc (*US sc*) in last dc (*US sc*), ss in first dc (*US sc*) (18).

Rnd 4: 1ch, 1dc (*US sc*) in same place as ss, 1dc (*US sc*) in next dc (*US sc*), (2dc/*US sc* in next dc/*US sc*, 1dc/*US sc* in each of next 2dc/*US sc*) five times, 2dc (*US sc*) in last dc (*US sc*), ss in first dc (*US sc*) (24).

Rnd 5: 1ch, 1dc (*US sc*) in same place as ss, 1dc (*US sc*) in each of next 2dc (*US sc*), (2dc/*US sc* in next dc/*US sc*, 1dc/*US sc* in each of next 3dc/*US sc*) five times, 2dc (*US sc*) in last dc (*US sc*), ss in first dc (*US sc*) (30).

Rnd 6: 1ch, 1dc (*US sc*) in same place as ss, 1dc (*US sc*) in each of next 3dc (*US sc*), (2dc/*US sc* in next dc/*US sc*, 1dc/*US sc* in each of next 4dc/*US sc*) five times, 2dc (*US sc*) in last dc (*US sc*), ss in first dc (*US sc*) (36).

Rnd 7: 1ch, 1dc (*US sc*) in same place as ss, 1dc (*US sc*) in each of next 4dc (*US sc*), (2dc/*US sc* in next dc/*US sc*, 1dc/*US sc* in each of next 5dc/*US sc*) five times, 2dc (*US sc*) in last dc (*US sc*), ss in first dc (*US sc*) (42).

Rnd 8: 1ch, 1dc (*US sc*) in same place as ss, 1dc (*US sc*) in each

Tip:
You can vary the size of the pond. If you want to make a bigger pond, simply add more rounds increasing stitches in the same manner.

of next 5dc (*US sc*), (2dc/*US sc* in next dc/*US sc*, 1dc/*US sc* in each of next 6dc/*US sc*) five times, 2dc (*US sc*) in last dc (*US sc*), ss in first dc (*US sc*) (48). Fasten off.

Filling the gaps

You can fill up the little gaps around the pond with rocks (see below). Or you can knit small triangle-shaped pieces by decreasing the stitches on one end at each row.

Materials

Rocks:

20g (¾oz) of grey or light brown yarn of your choice

Additional equipment

3mm (US C/2 or D/3, UK 11) crochet hook

Difficulty level

Beginner

Rocks

Using a grey yarn of your choice, cast on 4 sts, k 4 rows. Break yarn and draw through sts, pull tightly and fasten off. Using the yarn at the fasten-off end, sew the seam. Push in the other yarn end and close the cast-on end. You do not need extra stuffing. Sew the rocks around the pond.

Crochet clusters

Use grey DK (8-ply) yarn and a 3mm (US C/2 or UK D/3) hook. You can vary the number of stitches at random. Here are a few examples.

Treble cluster: (yarn round hook, insert hook in stitch, yarn round hook and pull up a loop, yarn round hook, pull loop through two loops) four to five times in the same st, yarn round hook, pull loop through all loops on hook.

Double treble cluster (US treble): (wrap yarn round hook twice, insert hook in stitch, yarn round hook and pull up a loop, yarn round hook, pull loop through first two loops, yarn round hook, pull loop through two loops) four to five times in same st, yarn round hook and pull loop through all loops on hook.

Tip:
You can vary the sizes of rocks by changing the stitch and row numbers. You can also use Aran (worsted) or chunky yarn, or knit the DK (8-ply) yarn double. Make crochet clusters instead of knitted rocks, if you prefer.